The Poetry, Art and Science of Psychoanalysis in Bion's 'O'

I0094990

The Poetry, Art and Science of Psychoanalysis in Bion's 'O' pays homage to Wilfred Bion's lifelong love of poetry and his desire to integrate it with his psychoanalytic work as a means of communicating profound levels of emotional experience.

Annie Reiner was a student of Bion in the 1970s in Los Angeles. She illustrates here the fundamental similarities in the states of mind of creative people across diverse disciplines in the Arts and Sciences to exemplify Bion's concept of 'O'. Reiner, herself a poet and artist, shows how psychoanalysis and poetry rely on the same tools – symbols, metaphors, images and narrative – to communicate and express otherwise inexpressible metaphysical matters of mental life. Focusing on key psychoanalytic ideas, such as dream interpretation and trauma, she weaves in the poetry of Rumi, Pablo Neruda, Fernando Pessoa and William Blake, and ideas of artists like Matisse, Rothko and Jackson Pollock, as well as ideas of Christian and Hindu mystics to show analysts how creative arts can help them better understand primitive mental life. She shows how examining ideas from other disciplines in the arts, philosophy and religious thought can reveal an underlying unity of our ancient efforts to understand ourselves as human beings.

Written in an accessible style and drawing on Reiner's decades of experience within the creative and psychoanalytic fields, this book is a valuable resource to all analysts in training and practice, as well as those interested in understanding the deeper levels of the mind and emotional life.

Annie Reiner is a senior faculty member and training analyst at The Psychoanalytic Centre of California (PCC) in Los Angeles, USA, and Fellow of the International Psychoanalytic Association. She lectures throughout the world and is published in numerous journals and anthologies. She is the author of three psychoanalytic books, *The Quest for Conscience and the Birth of the Mind* (2009), *Bion and Being: Passion and the Creative Mind* (2012) and *W. R. Bion's Theories of Mind: A Contemporary Introduction* (2022), and is the editor of *Of Things Invisible to Mortal Sight: Celebrating the Work of James S. Grotstein* (2016). Dr. Reiner maintains a psychoanalytic practice in Beverly Hills, California.

The Poetry, Art and Science of Psychoanalysis in Bion's 'O'

Annie Reiner

Routledge
Taylor & Francis Group

LONDON AND NEW YORK

Designed cover image: Annie Reiner, Jenny Okun, David Glynn

First published 2026
by Routledge
4 Park Square, Milton Park, Abingdon, Oxon OX14 4RN

and by Routledge
605 Third Avenue, New York, NY 10158

Routledge is an imprint of the Taylor & Francis Group, an informa business

For Product Safety Concerns and Information please contact our
EU representative GPSR@taylorandfrancis.com. Taylor & Francis
Verlag GmbH, Kaufingerstraße 24, 80331 München, Germany.

Trademark notice: Product or corporate names may be trademarks
or registered trademarks, and are used only for identification and
explanation without intent to infringe.

British Library Cataloguing-in-Publication Data
A catalogue record for this book is available from the British
Library

ISBN: 978-1-032-74794-1 (hbk)
ISBN: 978-1-032-74251-9 (pbk)
ISBN: 978-1-003-47095-3 (ebk)

DOI: 10.4324/9781003470953

Typeset in Times New Roman
by codeMantra

Contents

Permissions

Foreword

The following line was written by Jean Arp, the early 20th-century Dada artist and poet.

> May the daring eagle of dreams always protect your roses.
>
> (Arp, 1972, p. 279)

I cannot say I "understand" exactly what he had in mind, so I will not attempt to explain it, especially since, as Robert Frost (1961) wisely said, poetry is that which "is lost in translation" (p. 7). While the intellectual message may remain, the power of poetry to enter and touch the heart, soul, or mind is easily lost, for the medium – in this case the particular form and symbolic language of poetry – *is* the message.

We do not usually hear that Frost also said much the same thing about prose, thereby extending the mysteries and limitations of communication to the entire subject of language. Bion (1970) spoke often about the limitations of language in dealing with emotional states, which is especially significant for psychoanalysts, who have to use everyday language, largely created to deal with physical realities, to communicate about the much less tangible, metaphysical realities of mental life (cf. Reiner, 2022). The art of poetry faces similar challenges, and as I will discuss throughout this book, poetry's idiosyncratic use of language has much in common with the way analysts use language. Poetry's symbolic and metaphorical language can help us to *feel* its message rather than understanding it solely through reason and logic, which is also true of the symbolism of dreams, so central to the language of psychoanalysis. Bion wrote:

> The language of ordinary human beings is only appropriate to the rational, can only describe the rational, can only make statements in terms of rationality.
>
> (Bion, 1992, p. 371)

We will therefore examine the common language employed by psychoanalysts and poets, in their respective needs to communicate truths at deep levels of the personality beyond the rational.

Language is a complicated matter, for while it is easy for people to learn to speak, for words truly to have meaning, they have to emerge from a mind that can feel the reality of whatever those words seek to describe, which enables them to be felt by the other. Bion (1970) distinguished between the Language of Achievement, able to express the truth, including psychical states, and the Language of Substitution which uses substitutes to truth that impede true communication. The difference may not be readily apparent, but it nonetheless represents the essential distinction between using language in the service of truth or lies.

Just as psychoanalysis is designed to describe things beyond what we can physically see, hear or feel with our senses, poetry often expresses feelings and metaphysical realities that can only be read, as many poets have said, *between the lines.* This speaks to the complex challenge of finding a language able to express the realities of inner life, the passion, intensity and complexity of experiences that are beyond physical, sense-based experience. To do so, poems, like dreams, rely on symbols and metaphors that can *represent,* but never fully logically capture those realities. Psychoanalysts, poets and visual artists, all face this challenge of how to communicate profound, ephemeral realities that cannot be expressed in rational terms. It is also true in philosophy and religion. Christ expressed the same dilemma when he was asked by his disciples why he speaks in parables, using metaphorical, symbolic representations to express the matters of the spirit. He replied, "Because the mysteries of the kingdom…are not revealed to them" (Gospel of Matthew 13: 10–12). Christ therefore used parables in an effort to reach people who did not have "ears to hear" his metaphysical messages, or the "eyes" to see that which cannot actually be seen.

Although I cannot exactly translate Arp's poetic line above, I have a sense that whatever he is saying may very well be the point of this book. I think this is so in part because his paradoxical depiction of dreams as a strong, predatory eagle that can also protect something in us with the delicate beauty of a rose, makes some kind of emotional "sense" to me. It is not the "sense" of logical thought, but the intuitive sense that is fundamental to the creative Arts, and to psychoanalysis, as well as to other profound spiritual or religious perceptions. Arp's image echoes the central importance of dreams in Freudian theory and practice, as an enigmatic, but powerful, force of unconscious messages that might otherwise remain hidden from our logical minds. These thoughts, although unconscious, nonetheless have enormous power, with the potential for both positive and negative effects on our psyches, largely determined by whether or not we can become conscious of ideas that continue to confront us with the compelling strength and enigmatic beauty of our own unknown truths.

Dreams as unconscious thinking

There are significant differences between Freud's and Bion's notions of the Unconscious, some of which will be discussed in the book. One of them has to do with the purposes of dreaming, recognized by Freud to be "the royal road" to knowledge of unconscious mental states, but which Bion also viewed as an essential function in the development of the capacity to think. I thought this idea of dreaming was also vaguely implicit in Arp's image of our dreams as protectors. According to Bion (1962a), our dreams give form to proto-mental feelings and thoughts that our primitive minds experience, but cannot yet consciously feel or think. Dreaming is part of the development of Bion's (1962a) idea of "alpha function," the mind's capacity to transform emotional experiences into "alpha elements," which then become the building blocks of thoughts. Alpha elements, Bion (1962a) writes, "… resemble and may in fact be identical with the visual images with which we are familiar in dreams" (p. 7).

For Bion, in short, dreaming is the foundation of thinking. These dream-like mental functions are relevant to the subject of this book, because the dream's primal precursors to thinking – symbols, images, stories, intuited feelings and emotional truths – are what artists and writers, as well as psychoanalysts, rely upon to do their work.

I think we might also look at dreams as what Bion later described as "thoughts without a thinker," truths that exist in the world whether or not we are capable of knowing them, but which we might, through more primitive means, be able to dream them.

The poetic image of a "daring eagle of dreams," implies something able to soar weightless, much like imagination does. Imagination is an aspect of mental functioning that is as light and ephemeral as a dream, but which Arp's quote suggests may also have the power to safeguard our unique potential for a human mind. This seems to me to be a significant matter, as it becomes increasingly clear that the "rose," growing out of that potential for the ephemeral beauty and integrity of the human mind, is now very much in *need* of protection against the many erosive forces of ignorance, confusion, lies and unconsciousness. Those erosive forces exist both in ourselves and in the societies we have created throughout the world. We do seem currently to have entered a modern Dark Ages, with the possible threat of even darker consequences than in Medieval times. In the 1970s, Bion often called attention to the sometimes subtle compromises in our capacities for truth, morality and thinking, values long-held, and perhaps even taken for granted, which have since been overtly and alarmingly compromised in social and political discourse. These forces have always been present, of course, so while it may look as though we are devolving, what sadly seems more likely is that the human species as a whole may not yet have evolved sufficiently to know how to protect the beauty and delicacy of our mental "roses." This was Bion's view, for he often pointed out that mankind is still in its infancy, and that even our use of language as an essential tool for thought, is a mere 5,000 years old (Sumerian), or at most 7,000 years (Sanskrit). Bion wrote:

"Thinking", in the sense of engaging in that activity which is concerned with the use of thoughts, is embryonic even in the adult and has yet to be fully developed by the race.

(Bion, 1962a, p. 85)

It is not surprising, then, that seemingly basic knowledge about truth and lies, good and evil – the fundamentals of civilized discourse – are still not something upon which we can agree. I believe it is in part for this reason that Bion puts the word, "Thinking" in quotation marks in his statement above, because his theories of thinking call attention to a kind of mental functioning that differs from our commonly accepted beliefs about what thinking actually is. These are fundamental questions that Bion felt were necessary to ask about things we may believe we have already answered. This includes our assumed proficiency in language to express our assumed proficiency in thinking. As we will later see, Nietzsche (1888) often questioned similarly "obvious" beliefs, and noted the dangers in them, pointing out that, "Convictions are more dangerous enemies of truth than lies" (p. 134). We may become so convinced we know something, or so enamored by our knowledge and certainty, that we cannot make room for a new thought.

Unfortunately, the common view is more in line with what we now see as pervasive in society, people who are seemingly adept at using language, but use it in a way that is a mere facsimile of real thinking, while on a deeper level they remain unable to distinguish good from evil, or truth from lies, in themselves and others. In other words, as suggested in the oxymoron, "alternative facts," many of us are not really able to think, which Bion's painstaking theories of thinking were trying to address. What we call "thinking," he suggests, has not yet evolved to include the feelings and dreams that underlie and give meaning to our knowledge, and so what we call thinking remains a kind of ego-driven facsimile of thinking. In examining those underlying levels of truth through poetry and the Arts, I hope to provide a means to continue looking at this, and to revive our awareness of what Bion saw as essential to analytic work, and to the idea of absolute truth that he called O.

Clinical vignette

I will give a brief vignette about these issues of language, from my work with "Chloe," a patient who had been in analysis for just a few months, when this linguistic obstacle became evident. She is bright and intuitive, and presented with the complaint that her parents, who were seemingly very attentive, didn't really know who she was, and yet she felt it was impossible to separate from them, particularly her mother. Chloe embraced our work at first because she appreciated that someone was really listening to her and talking about things no one had ever talked to her about. However, I soon recognized times when I could not really get through to her, that she didn't really know what we were doing there. While this may be perfectly natural at the beginning of treatment, it is something we as analysts can too easily gloss over if we assume that we are speaking the same language as the patient. After another week or so Chloe began to miss seeing her mother, and feared that if she separated from her that she would have nothing. In subsequent sessions she admitted to feeling "stuck," to not wanting to do anything, including talk to me. I felt as if she were treading water, and in fact, she had a dream about being on a family vacation, where she and her mother were on the ocean in a leaky boat. I interpreted her terror of leaving her mother, as she had a sense that something in her was being born, and she did not know what, or who, that might be. We were also now felt to be in this dangerous leaky boat.

The next day was a continuation of Chloe's sense of being emotionally detached, and I eventually again addressed her uncertainty about whether she wanted to be emotionally born or not. She became silent for five to eight minutes, and seemed not to know how to respond. I said that I sensed she was confused about what I said, or why I was saying it, or what it meant. She agreed that she did not know what I meant. Of course, I considered that perhaps I was off the mark, but I did not think so, and when other things I said were also met with dead silence, I thought that she was now a very tiny newborn and I was the mother she did not trust to understand her. She did not even know what words were, if no one ever told her the truth about what she felt. I interpreted that she had put all her faith in her mother as an infant, and it had not worked out for her, and so she seems to feel safe only in the womb. If she is born, she does not even know what words are, or who she is, and she feels that I, as she has often said about her mother, will not know she exists at all. I said that it must then be frightening for she seems not to know today if she exists, and doesn't know if she should trust me to help. She remained silent until the end of the session.

The next day she came in and took up each of my interpretations, first saying that it was true that she did not understand my words, and did not know who she is. She had heard what I said about no one ever having told her the truth and so she does not really know what it is. She then "reassured" me, and/or herself, that she *did* know that she was there with me because she had some kind of disorder, and wanted help with it. I pointed out that while I understood that she knew *logically* why she was coming, I was talking about a different level of feeling in her that seemed *not* to know, and at that level she did not understand. We were both aware that she knew quite well how to talk, but if no one ever told her anything about herself that rang true, she cannot tell what it is I'm saying, or whether it is of any use to her. She admitted that she was afraid that she did not know what was going to happen with me. I assured her that this was a very real issue, and at this point there was no way for either of us to know what would happen, for it was in the future neither of us knew about now. All we could know was that right now, she is afraid that this new thing with me, with its very different kind of language, terrifies her. I said that I thought this was exactly where she should be, because at the moment, this is where she is. It was the first session that I felt her real self had actually been there with me.

What seemed encouraging to me about this session was that in her resistance, Chloe had dared to be where she actually was, to trust me enough to allow for the idea of a different reality about which she knew nothing, and about which we could then actually have a conversation. We had gotten by thus far using the common language that she had learned to speak in her family, a language devoid of feelings or truth. While this may be the language she, and many others, speak, that is not the language of psychoanalysis. These two sessions reflected the dream-like state that Bion denoted as O, the language of metaphysics, of dreams and of poetry. Because she did not yet know that language, she suddenly had no idea what I was talking about. Obviously she had to speak the only language she could thus far speak, although I could tell at a certain point that we could go no further like that. Still, we had to wait until these sessions in which this particular reality was ready to be born, which is the art and poetry of psychoanalysis.

Intelligence versus artificial intelligence

Some of these issues, and Bion's ideas about the mind, can also be seen in the growing concerns about the dangers of artificial intelligence (AI). AI is felt to be a threat to all kinds of artists, thinkers and philosophers whose works can be adapted and distorted mechanically to create something that cannot only be used to plagiarize the ideas and works of others, but which also bypass the human mind entirely. Bion's theories help us to think in new ways about what the mind actually is, and when, as quoted above, he characterized our current level of thinking as "embryonic," it helps us to consider the idea that what we commonly consider to be the mind is in many ways a form of "artificial intelligence," a substitute for intelligence that is based primarily on logic, bypassing what Bion saw as the *emotional* awareness that is the foundation of thinking. The development of the mind, and of thinking, always depends on our capacities to feel and to dream, which provide us with the building blocks for *rational thought.* It is a tricky enterprise indeed, especially if we believe we have already mastered rational thought when in fact we are just beginning that journey. Bion's message was clear – we are not there yet – and so rather than congratulating ourselves about all that we know, we need to start asking the many questions that may lead us to the vast realm of our own ignorance, from which we might start to learn more. We need first to stop reaching into that reassuring well of previously learned knowledge that makes us feel learned and wise, and free our minds to provide a space to see the new mystery in each moment. As with Chloe, one can go on speaking the old language that is known and comfortable but incapable of real communication, and growth, or one can dare to be quiet long enough to become curious, allowing the questions and the mystery to arise and meet us where we are. The importance of this is described by Bion's emphasis on imagination.

> On the way to being an analyst, you have to reserve the right to indulge your ... speculative imagination ... to give our imagination ... a chance to develop into something that might be scientific.
>
> (Bion, 1997, p. 47)

This is not to dismiss the assets of our prior knowledge, but to understand the ways in which our reliance on it, especially in clinical work, can obstruct further development.

Each of our own personal "artificial intelligence" is fed by that belief that we already know things we do not necessarily know, for without the ability to digest and process one's emotions so that they can be contained in thought, one's mind is more like a computer, or AI, that can store an enormous amount of data, but with no real sense of what it means. Knowledge begins with intuition and imagination, emotional capacity that finds its way to thoughts, something that poets and other artists know intuitively.

It seems that in spite of myself I have offered a kind of a long-winded "translation" or interpretation of Arp's line of verse. It includes the psychoanalytic idea that whether we know it or not, our ephemeral and mysterious dreams continue to carry the unvarnished truths that are fundamental to our mental growth. I think the point of Frost's idea of the elusiveness of translations is that, while translations may succeed in making logical sense to us, the special communicative power of poems to speak directly to one's emotional core derives from their idiosyncratic use of words born of something beyond logic. The poem itself often conveys the idea more effectively than logical, prosaic translations, for poems, like dreams, speak the language of the unconscious. They create their own language, just for that poem. As Frost described it, poetry is, "something dawning on you while you're writing it… you didn't think this all out" (Frost, 1961, p. 14). Like a dream, we make it up as we go along, without what we normally call "thinking."

Whether in a poem or story or other works of art, the artist's ability to enter the dream-like mind makes it possible for the reader to receive the underlying truth at that dream-like level, and it is this, I think, that cannot be translated. Keats similarly says:

> Poetry should be great and unobtrusive, a thing which enters into one's soul, and does not startle it or amaze it with itself but with its subject.
>
> (Keats, February 3, 1818)

I will examine in this book, the many means we have to speak directly from that dreaming mind, and *to* that dreaming mind. It is a means of protecting and developing our inherited potential for a human mind responsive to real thought derived from real feeling. According to Bion (1970), truth is the most essential mental need, without which the mind cannot grow and thrive. Just as the body needs food to survive, the mind needs truth, and the disciplines of poetry, art, science, psychoanalysis and religious thought have always been providers of that mental nourishment. Once contained or given form – whether in a poem, a story, a painting or a psychoanalytic interpretation – difficult or painful feelings can become less painful and less difficult, for they have become in some way more manifest. Arp's poetic statement includes the critical importance of our own enigmatic dreams as conveyers of truth. As I suspected, that is pretty much the point of this book, to explore how we can develop our own mental potential through these dream-like states that contain and sometimes mysteriously express deep wells of wisdom, otherwise overlooked. Like poems, the meanings of our dreams often elude our intellect, but they nonetheless continue to embody and communicate the true stories of our emotional lives that we ourselves may not necessarily know we are living.

References

Arp, J. (1972). *Arp on Arp*. New York: Penguin/Random House.

Bion, W. R. (1962a). *Learning from Experience*. New York: Basic Books.

Bion, W. R. (1970). *Attention and Interpretation*. London: Karnac.

Bion, W. R. (1992). *Cogitations*. London: Karnac.

Bion, W. R. (1997). In F. Bion (Ed.). *Taming Wild Thoughts*, 29 May 1977 (pp. 39–51) London: Karnac.

Frost, R. (1961). In C. Brooks; R. P. Warren (Eds.). *Conversations on the Craft of Poetry*. Conversation between Robert Frost, Cleanth Brooks, and Robert Penn Warren (pp. 3–18) New York: Hold Rinehart and Winston.

Gospel of Matthew: 13:10–12. In *The Jerusalem Bible, Reader's Edition*. New York: Doubleday & Company, Inc., 1968.

Keats, J. (February 3, 1818). Letter. In R. Adams (Ed.). (2017) *Art Can Help* (Frontispiece). New Haven, CT: Yale University Art Gallery.

Nietzsche, F. (1888). *The Will to Power*. New York: Vintage Books, 1967.

Reiner, A. (2022). *W.R. Bion's Theories of Mind: A Contemporary Introduction*. London: Routledge.

Introduction

Why poetry?

One of the reasons I wanted to write this book is that, as a poet, I had often thought of certain poets' works, whose sensitivity to emotional realities might be useful in teaching classes for psychoanalytic candidates. I had years ago written a paper on the language of the unconscious in both poetry and psychoanalysis (Reiner, 2008), and later used examples of different poets and artists to illuminate the psychoanalytic ideas in my book, *Bion and Being: Passion and the Creative Mind* (Reiner, 2012). However, I thought there was more to say on the subject, with the aim of approaching a more experiential sense of some psychoanalytic theories. This very much includes Bion's concept of O, his ideas about absolute truth and ultimate reality, whose meanings are obscured by a merely intellectual understanding. This Introduction is, in a sense, a preliminary introduction to this most elusive and controversial of Bion's ideas. Ultimately unknown and unknowable, O is the essence of experience, whether in psychoanalysis, art or religion, and each of these disciplines are useful in getting us closer to getting a sense of what this state of mind is, and its importance in all creative endeavors.

Bion's relationship to poetry

Another inspiration to writing this book reflects something I learned several years ago about Bion's avid interest in poetry. After Bion's death in 1979, his widow, Francesca, wrote, "Poetry was of central importance to him all his life" (Bion, 1981, Memorial, p. 3). She then noted that Bion had planned to publish an anthology of poems by his favorite poets, a collection of poems chosen specifically for psychoanalysts. He intended to use these poems, "Not for anyone who is merely called a psychoanalyst, not the label of certification, but the 'real thing'" (Bion, 1981, Memorial, p. 4). For Bion, the "real thing" or the *authentic* person or *authentic* experience, was associated with the idea of an on-going process of "becoming," whether one was becoming an analyst, a mother, a father, an artist or a human being. This continuous process of learning and change represented the on-going challenge of "becoming" one's true self and having one's own mind. Given our

DOI: 10.4324/9781003470953-1

finite minds and the infinite nature of unconscious mental life, it is a challenge that is never finished.

Ferenczi stressed the need for the analyst to be real, sincere and authentic, rather than placing himself in a falsely superior role of psychoanalyst. He writes, "The intellectual coolness of the analyst eventually provokes a kind of revolt" (Ferenczi, 1932, p. 56). Years later, Bion (1978a) similarly described the importance for an analyst to be "a human being," and not just "*representations* of a human being" (p. 367). Here and elsewhere, Bion discriminates between that aspiration toward authenticity and, "Good imitations of a psycho-analytic interpretation [that] produces artificial interpretations" (p. 367).

Bion's aim in presenting a book of poems seemed in part to underline his frustration about how to help analysts to continue *becoming* analysts, to avoid getting stuck in theories and in what one has already learned, so that one can keep learning in every session with every patient. Bion seemed to view poetry as an effective ambassador for invisible and profound realities of unconscious life. I will talk further about the reasons that poetry can more effectively illuminate the emotional mysteries of mental life that are represented in psychoanalytic understanding of the mind.

The impulse to put together such a book also reflected the importance that poetry held for Bion (1982a, 1982b) in his life. He expressed one reason for its importance in relation to his experience as a tank commander in WWI at the tender age of eighteen. He wrote about the horrifying carnage of war, witnessing his friends, young men under his command, being blown to bits right in front of him. In between the harrowing German attacks, Bion occupied himself by memorizing his favorite poems, an attempt, as he said, "to remain human". In speaking later about the horrendous effects of one vicious battle in Amiens, France in 1918, he said that while he and his cohorts may, "look so life-like, really we are dead. Oh yes, I died – on August 8th, 1918" (Bion, 1982a, p. 265).

The idea of poetry as a humanizing force may relate not only to the pleasure gained from the *content* of poetry as a mirror for our own deep emotional experiences, but also from the *form* of poetry, namely, its idiosyncratic use of language that enables the poet to contain and communicate the emotional essence of otherwise ineffable feelings. I think the humanizing effect of poetry to which Bion alluded derives from this capacity to use language in a way that engages both emotional and rational mental functions, a union of unconscious and conscious aspects of the mind that can put one in contact with a more integrated or evolved state of mind. This facilitates the capacity to use language in a way that can contain and think about emotional and metaphysical truths. Such communications provide a bridge between different aspects of one's own mind, that also enables one to create a bridge to connect one's mind to the mind of an Other in a shared emotional experience, like poetry.

This is based on Bion's idea of dreaming as the basis of thinking. This is in opposition to our usual assumption that thinking is first of all a logical endeavor. Our attempts at authentic emotional connection and communication, whether in psychoanalysis, poetry or art, are intimate reflections of our most primal needs for connection and love, and whatever obstacles we encounter to the satisfaction of those needs, which often result in disconnection and confusion.

The close connection between these very different activities of psychoanalysis and poetry may not be immediately obvious, but we have only to consider our dreams – Freud's "royal road" to unconscious processes of the mind – which are essentially poems. Dreams use the same tools as poetry – symbols, metaphors, images and narratives – to create and reveal complex ideas of which we are often completely unaware consciously. In fact, they do it without any apparent help from us, since we concoct these elaborate creations while we are sound asleep. Both poems and dreams speak fluently the language of the unconscious. Our waking minds lack this particular talent, and this is very much at the heart of Bion's idea of O as necessary in doing analytic work.

Creativity and Bion's 'O'

Bion's work has inspired my psychoanalytic and mental growth for over four decades. In roughly that same time period, my other inspirations, aspirations and obsessions have included poetry, art, and philosophy, for having become a painter, playwright and a poet in my early thirties, I found striking similarities in my experiences of each of these very different endeavors. I noticed a kind of communication between them in my mind, for each of them helped me to understand and work with the others. This included my practice of psychoanalysis, for in writing and painting, I spent a lot of time in my own unconscious mind, which made it possible for me to tune into that deep level of my patients' minds. The unconscious creates specific demands on one's psyche and as one gets more familiar with what that feels like, one also strengthens one's ability to tolerate and experience the mystery of one's own mind, as well as those of the patient. Specifically, it means being able to set aside one's impatience, and what Bion called one's memory and desire, in order to experience the actual experience of the patient. It is what Bion called at-one-ment with O, whether it is at-one-ment with one's own emotional reality, or with that of the patient. For Bion, this is the critical state of mind for doing psychoanalytic work, for one cannot really experience something in someone else's mind that one has never experienced in one's own.

Given the intertwining lessons I learned from these other disciplines, it was no surprise to me that Bion wrote:

> It would be useful if we could recognize that all these various disciplines – music, painting, psychoanalysis and so on ad infinitum – are engaged on the same search for truth.
>
> (Bion, 1978b, 1978c, p. 43)

The common denominator is truth, so while each of these disciplines differs in form, content and means of communication, the search for, and apprehension of truth remains the same. As Bion (1982b) also said, "…[B]y 'truth' I mean 'aesthetic' truth and 'psychoanalytic' truth: this last I consider to be a 'grade' of scientific truth" (Preface, p. 8).

Not only do the forms and methods used in each of these fields differ, they differ for each artist, and often change over time even in the works of one artist. Picasso is a good example, for while we can see that the form of his more classically inspired early paintings is fundamentally different from the forms of his later Cubist or expressionistic works, they all bear the stamp of his capacity for aesthetic truth, and emotional truth. One may not be able to say what that truth is, but one can feel whether or not something real and meaningful is being expressed. The same is evident for Picasso's friend and competitor, Matisse, whose work Picasso admired more than all his contemporaries. Despite the fact that his aesthetic truth was so different from Picasso's, it was certainly no less true (Gilot, 1990). Like one's unique fingerprints or DNA, individual artists' aesthetics differ from each other, and while each artist's style may continue to evolve, the fingerprint is still there. The aesthetic truth is a constant. Each painting, if it is to be meaningful and satisfying to the artist himself, and to the viewer, must be true to the painter who paints it. The same is true in psychoanalysis. Analysts have their own styles, based on their different personalities, different experiences and different minds, so they will inevitably work differently, but despite these fundamental differences, the work, if it is to be effective, must bear its own corresponding stamp of truth.

The danger exists that one will be such a good student of one's analyst or supervisors that one's work may bear the stamp of someone else's fingerprints. Bion was familiar with the danger of this, as we see in these words by Meltzer.

> …psychoanalytic training has had an oppressive effect upon Bion. It is perhaps one of the great limitations of this sort of training that the personal analysis takes so long to 'recover from', to use a phrase Bion employed in 1976 in his lecture at the Tavistock Centre.
>
> (Borgogno; Merciai, 2000, p. 76)

Meltzer goes on to say that all of Bion's major writings were published after the death of his analyst, Melanie Klein, in 1960, suggesting that these influences, while helpful, may be difficult to move beyond. When I met with Bion (1977) to set up a private clinical seminar, he said something very similar to me, "Every analyst must find one's own language… only after one's analysis has ended."

Finding one's own style and one's own language may be difficult to identify or describe in any field. Emily Dickinson did a pretty good job of it, however, in a conversation she had about poetry with Thomas Wentworth Higginson, a writer and clergyman to whom she sent her poems after having read something he wrote to encourage new writers. He was the first, among very few, who had praised or supported Dickinson's poetry, and in their first meeting, he asked her how she knows what a poem is.

If I read a book and it makes my whole body so cold no fire can ever warm me, I know that is poetry. If I feel physically as if the top of my head were taken off, I know that is poetry.

(Dickinson, 1870, pp. 19–20)

While not everyone feels things as deeply as Dickinson, it is worth asking how one recognizes or accesses that experience of truth or authenticity in poetry, or in any field, including psychoanalysis.

While the expressions of truth in these diverse fields require different talents, each of them includes its own challenging mental discipline that helps facilitate access to one's own intuitive, dream-like state that provides entry into an intuitive realm of the mind. While related to Freud's idea of the Unconscious, the differences between that and Bion's concept of 'O' will be discussed throughout this book. This psychoanalytic concept of O is similar to what artists and writers describe as an empty mind, or Buddhists who describe this emptied mind as an egoless state in order more fully to inhabit the present moment. This is in keeping with Bion's idea of freeing one's mind of memory (the past), and desire (the future), leaving one in the present. This state is essential to what enables the artist to face the "blank page" or "blank canvas" that may strike fear in the writer or painter as one transitions from one's focus on the known physical world, to an unknown, dream-like, metaphysical world. It can be very unpleasant, especially at first, requiring patience and a kind of faith, until one learns that if one can bear it, one is rewarded with something new, whether a painting, a poem or story, or a psychoanalytic interpretation that embodies qualities of meaning, vitality, and truth. While I don't think I feel the top of my head being taken off when creating an interpretation, it is accompanied by a distinct and intuitive sense of something that feels right. One cannot manufacture that feeling, and my experience as an analyst is that if it is *not* there, whatever I may try to say feels like it is not worth saying.

Throughout this book, Bion's concept of O will be examined with reference to poems and psychoanalytic theories, but we can start with Bion's representation of O as an infinite and absolute truth or ultimate reality, and the state of mind by which this reality might be intuited. He describes its fundamental aspect in terms of Kant's idea of a numinous "thing-in-itself" that can never fully be known.

In any object, material or immaterial, resides the unknowable ultimate reality, the 'thing-in-itself'. Objects have emanations or emergent qualities or evolving characteristics that impinge upon the human personality as phenomena.

(Bion, 1970, p. 87)

He distinguishes here between the noumenon, an experience of metaphysical reality and the physical reality of phenomena.

When the noumena, the things themselves, push forward so far that they meet an object which we call the human mind, there then comes into being the domain of phenomena.... Corresponding to these phenomena... is the thing itself, the noumenon... The religious man would say... 'God.' What Freud and psycho-analysts have investigated is phenomena.

(Bion, 1974a, p. 41)

Bion is clear here that with his idea of O, one is studying a different domain of expe-rience than Freud or Klein, for which the analyst has to use a different aspect of the mind. In distinguishing the realms of noumenon and phenomenon, he describes the need for contact with the mysterious metaphysical reality different from our every-day relationship to the physical, rational and known world of everyday life. Bion's idea is not antithetical to Freud's Unconscious, which certainly described a timeless realm of mysteries, but the means of examining it at the time were often more lim-ited to logical discourse *about* this mysterious realm, rather than being submerged in it, or being one with it. It is something like the difference between being in a boat in the middle of the ocean, and swimming in the ocean with nothing but one's mind to help one stay afloat. It is not to say that there were no daring swimmers who plunged right into this unknowable ocean, but those who did, like Ferenczi, for instance, were often at odds with Freud and his followers. In a way, Bion's idea seeks to deepen our understanding, and our access, to this very different world of the mind, by trying to find a way to stay afloat in this vast and very different world.

This is why Bion warned of the potential dangers of contact with O, a kind of deep dive into boundless mental waters. Since contact with the waking-dream state of O means emptying one's mind of memory, desire and understanding, it is essentially a way of suspending use of these ego functions and surrendering to an egoless (oceanic) state. Bion (1970) pointed out that this could be "felt as a very serious attack on the ego," unless one's primitive paranoid-schizoid and depres-sive anxieties had already been effectively analyzed. One might then have learned how to manage the primitive feelings associated with the loss of one's familiar self (Bion, 1970, p. 48). While O proved to be Bion's most mysterious and contro-versial concept, it represents the state of mind that is the essence of all creativity, whether in the Arts or Sciences or religious philosophies. It is this paradoxical state of mindfulness and mindlessness that will be examined throughout this book with reference to works from these different disciplines.

Bion's introduction to his book of poems

Unfortunately, Bion never got around to putting together that book of his favorite poems for psychoanalysts, but the following statement is an excerpt from its Intro-duction, that Bion had already written before his death in 1979.

It is easy in this age of the plague – not of poverty and hunger, but of plenty, surfeit and gluttony – to lose our capacity for awe... I resort to the poets because they seem to me to say something in a way which is beyond my powers and yet to be said in a way which I myself would choose if I had the capacity. The unconscious – for want of a better word – seems to me to show the way 'down to descend', its realms have an awe-inspiring quality.

(Bion, 1981)

That sense of awe suffused Bion's work. It is an essential element of several of his contributions to psychoanalysis, but is most directly delineated in his concept of O. Our trepidation about this vast and transcendent feeling of awe seems to reflect our fears of our own insignificance, our limitations and our ignorance before this experience of the infinite. The controversies, and often the aversion to O among some analysts, is sometimes attributed to the connection Bion makes between O and mystical states, which are mistakenly confused with the traditional dogma of religious beliefs and institutions. What it really represents is that sense of awe that Bion felt we were in danger of losing. Religion is felt by some not to belong in psychoanalysis, as if it is somehow unscientific, a domain of sloppy or magical thinking. But again, I think it is the fear of that infinite unknown, and the attendant sense of awe, that is at the heart of the aversion to O. I will later talk further about Einstein's, and other scientists' ideas about religion, but will here cite just one thing he said on the subject.

The most beautiful and most profound emotion we can experience is the sensation of the mystical, it is the sower of all true science.

(Einstein, 1948, p. 117)

This will be discussed in Chapter 3, when we deal with ideas about the mystic through the works of mystical poets like Rumi and Hafiz, among others. But what Einstein is expressing here is the sense of awe at what we do not, and cannot, know, an awareness that is certainly relevant to science, as well as religious feeling. Without this perspective on the unknown, the psychoanalyst cannot reflect on deeper levels of a mind that does not give up its secrets easily.

It is worth mentioning that this sense of awe is also the natural domain of the infant, for whom every single thing is brand new, vastly mysterious, unknown, unknowable, and in a word, awesome. The normal, unbounded, infant mind in many ways *is* O, the seat of pure emotional experience, and oneness, in a mind as yet untethered and uncontained by thought and reason. Bion wrote:

The infant is somehow so highly intelligent that it is capable of seeing the vastness of its problems, but is without any equipment with which to deal with it.

(Bion, 1974b, CW, VII: 144)

The infant feels the vastness of its experiences in general, by which it is easily overwhelmed, and without a safe holding environment/mother, that child *will* be overwhelmed, by its own undigestible feelings. As adults, it is challenging, and can be dangerous, to allow ourselves to drop down into that primal mind, and yet this is essentially what Bion suggested was necessary in doing psychoanalytic work.

This is not to suggest that the infant experience is equivalent to the psychoanalyst's experience of O, or that babies can make good analysts, for while analytic work requires this primal perspective, it also requires the foundation of a more evolved and individuated mind that has learned to feel *and* think.

It is my understanding that Bion intended his book of poetry to present just the poems themselves, his favorite poems that meant the most to him. I am not certain just what he had in mind, but my book will not only be different poets, but I will also provide discussions of some of them in relation to the perspectives of psychoanalytic thought, as well as philosophical and religious thought. In addition to poems, and excerpts of poems, by Blake, Dickinson, Valéry, Rumi, Hafiz, Leopardi, Pessoa and others, I will also include some of my own poems, some of which are informed by my work as an analyst. Discussions of some of the works and writings of artists like Matisse, Rothko, Arp, and Pollack will help provide diverse perspectives on uncannily similar states of mind. The Arts often evoke more direct lines of communication to unconscious states, that can give us some help in finding ways to remain open to the sense of awe that Bion described.

References

Bion, F., Segal, H., Menzies-Lyth, I., & Meltzer, D (1981). *Memorial Meeting for Dr. Wilfred Bion. International Review of Psychoanalysis*, 8: 3–14.

Bion, W. R. (1963). *Elements of Psychoanalysis*. New York: Basic Books.

Bion, W. R. (1970). *Attention and Interpretation*. London: Karnac.

Bion, W. R. (1974a). Rio de Janeiro Lectures. In C. Mawson (Ed.). *The Complete Works of W.R. Bion*, Vol X: 74–75. London: Karnac, 2014.

Bion, W. R. (1974b). Sao Paulo Lectures. In C. Mawson (Ed.). *The Complete Works of W.R. Bion*, Vol VII: 71–197. London: Karnac, 2014.

Bion, W. R. (1977). *Private Conversation*. Bion's Office, 435 N., Bedford Dr., Beverly Hills, CA.

Bion, W. R. (1978a) August 1978). In F. Bion (Ed.) *Cogitations*, London: Karnac, 1992.

Bion, W. R. (1978b). Seminar 5, 4 July, 1978. In F. Bion (Ed.). *The Tavistock Seminars* (pp. 53–56). London: Karnac, 2005.

Bion, W. R. (1978c). *Four Discussion with W. R. Bion*. Perthshire: Cluny Press.

Bion, W. R. (1982a). *The Long Weekend 1897–1919: Part of a Life*. Abingdon: Fleetwood Press.

Bion, W. R. (1982b). *Preface. The Long Weekend 1897–1919: Part of a Life*. Abingdon: Fleetwood Press.

Dickinson, E. (1870). Conversation with Thomas Wentworth Higginson. In R. N. Linscott (Ed.). *Selected Poems and Letters of Emily Dickinson* (pp. 19–20). New York: Anchor Books/Doubleday, 1969.

Einstein, A. (1948). In L. Barnett (Ed.). *The Universe and Dr. Einstein* (p. 117). New York: A Mentor Book, The New American Library.

Ferenczi, S. (1932). *The Clinical Diary of Sándor Ferenczi*. In J. Dupont (Ed.); M. Balint, N. Z. Jackson (Trans.). Cambridge, MA: Harvard University Press, 1988.

Gilot, F. (1990). *Matisse and Picasso: A Friendship in Art.* New York: Doubleday.
Reiner, A. (2008a). The language of the unconscious: Poetry and psychoanalysis. *The Psychoanalytic Review*, 95: 4; 597–624.
Reiner, A. (2012). *Bion and Being: Passion and the Creative Mind.* London: Karnac

Chapter 1

Poems for psychoanalysts

Who was she who made love to you
in your dream, while you slept?
Where do the things in dreams go?
Do they pass to the dreams of others?
And does the father who lives in your dreams
die again when you awaken?
In dream, do plants blossom
and their solemn fruit ripen?
                    (Neruda, 2003, p. 43)

This poem is from Pablo Neruda's, *The Book of Questions*, a fitting title given the mysterious nature of dreams. It is fitting as well in view of Bion's own tireless curiosity, not just about dreaming but about almost everything pertaining to the mind, including the existence of the mind itself. In a private clinical seminar, Bion (1978) advised our group, "Always keep your questions in good repair." He often stressed his belief that continuing to ask questions was more important than our often insatiable hunger for answers.

Neruda here seems to be asking – "What are dreams?" – a question that psycho-analysts have addressed since Freud began his explorations of the mind. Like so many things, however, we may start to take our knowledge of dreams for granted, although Bion did ask new questions about dreams that opened our minds to new ideas. Neruda's poem reflects that kind of open mind able to wonder about the infinite world of dreams that we visit every night, and which often seem more real than reality. Among Bion's new ideas about dreams is the perception that they are the foundation of our capacity to think, even referring to dreams as "uncon-scious thinking." Dreaming, he noted, is not limited to our nighttime excursions, but rather is an ever-present function of our waking minds that continues to help us process and digest our feelings and thoughts. We are always dreaming, in other words, but the lack of stimulation when we're asleep makes our dreams a bit easier to see at night.

Neruda's questions give voice and form to this mysterious dreaming mind which impacts our relationships to reality, time and space. Dreams seem alien to

DOI: 10.4324/9781003470953-2

our waking minds, but make us aware of this other, and very different, reality that reflects who we are in a very important way. Poetry can be equally mysterious to people as dreams, for both provide evidence of how our minds work on their own, without our conscious control, often revealing a source of knowledge and wisdom that is otherwise unfamiliar to us. If we can tap into it, we may get help in "thinking" in ways that are emotional rather than logical, organic and innovative rather than formulaic or theoretical.

A word about poetry

Since we will be examining the similarities in the languages of poetry and psychoanalysis, it is important to note that there are many different kinds of poetry, ranging from limericks and doggerel to epic, Romantic, Symbolist and mystical poems, and everything in between. It is safe to assume that this discussion does not apply to all of them. The same range of diversity is obviously also present in the variety of genres of music and visual art but, as mentioned in the Introduction, some very diverse styles may share the common need to communicate some kind of truth. Different *levels* of truth are sought, however, whether in life or in art, and in the various kinds of psychotherapy and psychoanalysis that focus on different levels of mental experience. Some mental health practitioners deal with practical matters of living; others, like Cognitive Behavioral Therapists, seek to engage rational, cognitive mental functions, with the aim of reducing patients' symptoms. In general, psychoanalysts focus on the unconscious meanings of those symptoms, on metaphysical matters of the mind, to uncover deeply held but hidden beliefs that nonetheless deeply affect people's states of mind and behavior. And yet even within psychoanalysis there are significant differences in orientation, training and clinical methodology.

I would count myself among those on the psychoanalytic lineage of Freud, Klein, Bion, Object Relations and many contemporary analysts who typically address more primitive levels of psychic life than some other analysts. My focus in this book is on the kinds of artistic endeavors that communicate at equivalent levels of depth as psychoanalysis of this kind. Poets of this kind, for instance, often provide insights into fundamental emotional, psychical and philosophical truths, that may reveal something about unconscious states. This includes poets who wrote long before the discovery of psychoanalysis, some mystical or religious poets like Rumi and Hafiz, and later visionary poets like William Blake and Giacomo Leopardi, as well as more modern poets like Emily Dickinson, Paul Valéry and Fernando Pessoa. I have elsewhere included discussions of some poems by Rilke, Neruda, e. e. cummings and others (Reiner, 2012), whose works are not necessarily religious or mystical per sé, but which illuminate these same deep levels of psychical experience. This awareness has no time frame, however, for it has existed always in the minds of artists, philosophers and religious thinkers engaged in trying to figure out what it means to be human, with our specifically human potential for consciousness. In a letter to the writer, Roman Rolland, Freud himself expressed his belief that artists and writers are often more in touch with deeply unconscious thought processes than analysts. He said to Roland, whom he greatly admired, "Mysticism is just as closed to me as music… It is easier for you [writers] than for us [psychoanalysts] to read the human soul" (E. Freud, 1960, p. 388). We will examine some reasons for this in relation to the waking dream state of Bion's (1965, 1970) concept of O, that he saw as essential to psychoanalytic work.

The same psychological and philosophical questions of mental life have been central to ancient artists and thinkers as far back as the writers of religious texts in Hindu, Buddhist, Judeo-Christian and Muslim works, whose concerns were the fundamental truths that drive human beings, and yet often defy our attempts at description. It is, therefore, no surprise that these ideas have often bred confusion, controversy and even wars, both philosophical and physical. Nor is it surprising that poetry is a difficult path for poets whose works plumb similarly profound depths that are unfamiliar, and so threatening, to many. Writing in the early 1900s, the great Italian poet, Giacomo Leopardi, wrote that his century was not what he would call poetic, something that is undoubtedly even more true for us today.

> Everyone wants to write poetry, but prefers reading prose. And you know this century is not and cannot be poetic. A poet, even a great one, attracts little attention, and even if he gains fame in his own country it is hard for his reputation to spread…because perfect poetry cannot be carried over into foreign language, and because Europe wants something more solid than poetry.
>
> (Leopardi, 1826/1997, Frontispiece)

This is probably even more true in the 21st century than it was when Leopardi wrote this, for we are increasingly bombarded by distractions, both entertaining and technological, that leave little space and time for contemplation that facilitates these deeper states of mind. While there are many people in America and throughout the world who still love poetry, it is far from our entertainment of choice. Prose, more logical and straightforward, is preferred to the mysteries and uncertainties of poetry. The same can be said about psychoanalysis, with its ephemeral world of unconscious dreams, and its reputation for being slow, or ineffective, compared to more goal-oriented treatments with more logical and comprehensible perspectives on the "real" world, and methods that promise quicker results. This includes, of course, the prevalence, some analysts would say "epidemic" presence of psychotropic medications whose results are to be expected within weeks.

From its beginnings, psychoanalysis posed challenges to sociocultural beliefs, sometimes seen as shocking, and vaguely prurient. It did have its heyday around the 1950s, when Freud's methods and ideas permeated the society, offering hope of deeper understanding and even changing many of the long-held mores of oppressive and Victorian belief systems. It was the gold standard of mental health methods, and was soon accepted, to some extent, in cultures throughout the world. That changed, partly due to the typical length of treatment, but I fear also, because it hardened, like most institutionalized methods, into something less potent that its potential in its early stages of growth. Bion's determination to keep asking questions in the face of ossifying theoretical dogma, was an important part of his influence in psychoanalysis, and so while his ideas were based on Freud's, they demanded that we continue building on those ideas and growing new knowledge. He also helped to uncover this tendency of ideas to ossify within Institutions.

Given the complexity of the subject matter – the human mind – it is not surprising that psychoanalysis is still considered uncomfortably deep and mysterious, and maybe still even vaguely prurient. In addition, analytic treatment today is usually far longer than the relatively short analyses of Freud and his early colleagues, which sometimes lasted just months. It is understandable, because despite Freud's (1937) concerns expressed in *Analysis Terminable and Interminable*, as to whether or not there was such thing as a natural end, and how to accelerate a slow process, as analysts began addressing more and more primitive states of mind in their patients, it is not unusual for an analysis to last ten or fifteen years or more.

A lot has been learned about the mind in a century and a quarter since Freud, and it is an understatement to say that we have a lot more to learn. It seems particularly important now to learn from the diverse disciplines that have examined human consciousness since Freud, since we are living in a time when the very ideas of truth and consciousness have been degraded, if not lost, in parts of modern society. It is a dangerous trend, and one that psychoanalysis is particularly equipped to examine. The artists and thinkers that went before us, and those who have journeyed alongside psychoanalysis, are useful because understanding these mysteries of the mind entails not only the *content* of what we already know, but the different *forms* by which the creative arts can help convey these often dream-like realities.

The role of poetry in modern society

In general, poetry has taken a back seat to other, more linear forms of art and entertainment, which reflects some of the same difficulties people have in accessing deeper aspects of emotional life. Psychoanalysts can now recognize that many people have not developed the underpinnings of a self or mind that can feel that essential level of experience that is the domain of poetry and psychoanalysis. The overwhelming trend to prescribe more and more psychological medications promises to provide easier and faster ways to deal with painful feelings. Bion (1992) called drugs, "substitutes employed by those who cannot wait" (p. 299). Becoming accustomed not to wait is in direct opposition to that which is needed to develop a mind able to think about, and tolerate, frustrating and painful feelings. One is essentially divested of one's own feelings and so, from a psychoanalytic perspective, the cure becomes the illness.

There are notable exceptions to the trend away from poetry, certainly in Ireland, whose traditional love of poetry seems still to endure as part of their heritage. Before my first trip to Dublin about twenty years ago, I asked an artist friend who had spent time there, where I could go to hear poetry. He replied, "Just go up to anyone on the street and ask, 'Where's poetry?'" He turned out to be right, and I found on occasion that people actually came up to me and asked, "Would you like to hear a poem?" Instead of playing music, street artists might recite a poem by Seamus Heany or Patrick Cavanaugh, and one young man, after reciting a poem by his favorite poet, asked if I wanted to hear a poem that he wrote. It is hard to imagine something like that happening on American streets, but despite these variations in different societies, the plight of poetry cannot be ignored, especially when compared to the hallowed importance it held in the past.

Epic poets like Homer and Virgil were the historians of their day, and throughout the centuries poets were also seen as guardians of morality, voices of the divine. Renaissance poets held exalted positions as leaders and teachers, and Tromly (1968) describes what was believed to be "…the great responsibility upon the Poet's shoulders [as] a master of all knowledge" (p. 4). Long before that, Plato wrote:

> A poet is a light and wingéd thing, and holy… [T]he deity has bereft [poets] of their senses and uses them as ministers… in order that we listeners may know… that it is the god himself who speaks, and through them to become articulate to us…. Poets are nothing but interpreters of the gods.
>
> (Plato, 37 B.C.E., p. 220)

In essence, Plato is saying that God took away the logical minds of poets so they could better express His. This God-mind is also at the center of Bion's revolutionary idea of 'O,' representing absolute truth, ultimate reality and the Godhead, which will be discussed in Chapter 3. Bion viewed this perspective on the infinite as the necessary state of mind in doing psychoanalytic work.

Poetry and psychoanalysis

Part of our need for poetry, and for psychoanalysis, derives from the fact that metaphysical mysteries of mental life cannot really be expressed in our normal everyday language. Bion spoke often about the limitations of our language, derived from the *physical* world of the senses but which analysts have to use in communicating *metaphysical* realities of mental life. While each of these disciplines uses its own idiosyncratic mode of language to achieve their respective goals, their languages are also intimately connected. We see this clearly in the central role of dreams in early psychoanalytic theory and practice, Freud's (1900) "royal road to a knowledge of the unconscious activities of the mind" (p. 608). Like poetry, the language of dreams is based on symbols, metaphors and associations that even the dreamers themselves do not understand, which gives them both access to a metaphysical realm of emotional life. It also gives both poetry and dreams their ambiguous quality, even to the poets or dreamers who created them. As Browning famously said about a poem he had written:

> Once only God and Robert Browning knew what this poem meant, now only God knows.
>
> (Welles et al., 1998)

Browning's statement reflects the mysterious provenance of a poem, even one's *own* poem, which may appear in a flash as fleeting as lightning, which is gone in seconds. Its sense of "otherness" may make it appear to have written itself, or with the help of some otherworldly "Muse" or "God." Poets and other artists often view this as an external entity, when in fact it is a creation of the artist's unconscious that is unfamiliar to the waking mind. The same is true of a dream, which also sometimes appears and disappears in seconds, and also feels like a message from an unknown world unfamiliar to one's waking self.

The psychoanalyst's capacity for access to O, facilitates contact with those mysterious, intuitive sparkles of light or energy from the dreaming mind. In focusing on Bion's concept of O throughout the book, we will examine ways in which those flashes of lightning can be cultivated through waking dream states like the ones from which they came.

Some of my own poems feel like snapshots of those metaphysical realities, perspectives on that amorphous realm of dream energies. Like Browning's experience of his own poems as unknown to him, poems over which he has no conscious control, they are written in language different from the one we speak during the day. This poem came to me in a similar way, and seems to suggest this idea.

Gravity

Gravity connects sun and moon to earth,
connecting moments of time
which fall together to make a life,
as letters fall together to make words
falling together to make perfect poems
by poets falling apart.
                              (Reiner, 2008, p. 12)

Both poems and dreams are probably better able to embody a deeper logic whose meaning is implicit and elusive, and hopefully we can listen to them well enough to learn their language. With O, Bion suggests we find a way to invite our dreams into waking life.

One of the gifts derived from poetry, and from dreaming, is a capacity to bring unity to our divided minds, as they create a partnership between unconscious dream states and the conscious mind that may hear, record and remember the dream. Bion described this as the need for a sort of emotional binocular vision, an ability simultaneously to use one's binary mental functions, so that, "the conscious and the unconscious… function as if they were binocular therefore capable of correlation and self-regard" (1962, p. 54).

Although we will focus on the works of Rumi and other mystical poets in Chapter 3, I include this one here because it bears directly on this idea of an integration of disparate mental functions.

[W]e are bound for the depths
of space...
We've been in orbit before
and know the angels there...
Yet we are beyond all that
and something more than angels.
Out beyond duality,
we have a home, and it is Glory.
That pure substance is
different from this dusty world.
What kind of place is this?
(Rumi, 1981, p. 3)

What is this mind "beyond duality"? Of course, it is only metaphorically a "place," for the mind has no physical reality. Rather, I think it reflects the fluctuating energies of those two functions of dreaming and knowing. These are the same fluctuating energies Bion (1962) alludes to in his idea of a relationship between container and contained (♀♂), that allows us to bridge the gap between our two very different mental functions. Bion (1963) states, however, that each can act in the capacity of the other, again, a sense of union or integration "beyond duality."

[T]he two mechanisms (♀♂) can each operate in its characteristic manner or in a manner typical or reminiscent of the manner of operation of the other.
(Bion, 1963, p. 43)

Poetry as our first language

According to Bion, dreaming is the basis of our capacity to think, and so a necessary part of mental development. In a sense, this unconscious function of dreams is our first language, communications of raw emotional experiences before we are able to think. Every night, unwittingly, unconsciously, and while sound asleep, we create dreams, utilizing the same tools as poetry – symbols, metaphors, imagery, narratives and characters, thereby making each of us a natural poet (Reiner, 2008). However, we rarely understand our own dreams at first, or sometimes, as Browning said, our own poetry, for both are challenging mental disciplines that seem fairly alien to us when awake. When asleep, although, we have no problem crafting these dramatic mini-productions, poetic creations of uncanny depth and meaning that we cannot understand. The job of the psychoanalyst is to help patients to understand something of their own mental productions by decoding the symbols they unconsciously created by themselves, which provide knowledge as to where and who one is at the moment. The psychoanalyst has to be something of a poet, working backwards to *feel* the essence of the patient's poetic dream-state that created the imagery and symbols. In a sense, the analyst has to dream the patient's dream, which is what Bion means when he says that "… the psychoanalytic vertex is O" (p. 27). The psychoanalytic perspective is the analyst's ability to enter and engage with that dream state, while awake.

The challenges of this mental discipline will be examined throughout this book. Whether for our patients or ourselves, it is worth noting that although these are our own productions, they often seem to come from somewhere or someone else. And in a way they may do just that, for the unconscious is that mysterious "place" with no actual location, from which many, if not most, people are estranged, and with which it is difficult to reengage.

Dreams are enormously complex, however, for we may also absorb the energies of those around us, in the past and the present, which also find their way into one's dream. It is difficult then to determine the origin and composition of a dream.

Historical notions of dreams

Throughout history, people have theorized and conjectured about what dreams are. Grotstein (2000) notes that Assyrians viewed dreams as "a secret language between the gods" (p. 28). Other theories range from prophecies of future events – like Joseph's Biblical interpretations of Pharoah's dreams (Genesis: 41–50) – to Freud's (1950) ideas of dreams as symbolic representations of hidden, often unacceptable, repressed unconscious impulses. Their meanings might be gleaned through the techniques Freud (1900) set out in *The Interpretation of Dreams*, and from the innovations about dreaming that Bion (1962, 1963, 1970) described as precursors to the development of thinking. Although we will examine these and other ideas about dreaming, this is not an extensive history of dreams, for the aim is to look at dreaming as a central and essential aspect of mental life that has great significance in psychoanalytic ideas of the mind, that are also reflected in the creative states of mind in all areas of life.

It seems clear to me, however, that dreams can be different things at different times, or mixtures of various mental functions and ideas concurrently. To use one Old Testament myth as an example, Joseph's interpretations of Pharoah's dream about seven fat cows and seven lean cows are presented both as symbolic *and* prophetic. Joseph interpreted the fat cows as symbols of seven years of plenty, and the lean cows as symbols of seven years of famine, but this symbolic meaning was also viewed as a *prediction* of what was about to happen in Egypt. The story is that Pharaoh took Joseph's prophecy to heart, using his interpretation to prepare for the future by storing food in the years of plenty, to sustain the country in the lean years that followed, as Joseph predicted.

While I know of no proof that this Biblical myth is historically accurate, it serves as a way to discuss these different views of dreaming, both of which I have had evidence in patients' dreams. The myth suggests that Joseph had the gift of prophecy, an extraordinary intuition which proved valuable enough to Pharaoh that he appointed Joseph, formerly a servant in Pharaoh's army, to be "governor of the whole land of

Egypt," second only to Pharaoh (Exodus: 41:41). Again, this is not a comment on the historical accuracy of Joseph's prophetic gift, but on the beliefs about dreams. I have seen people in my practice, however, who do have this uncanny intuitive gift, and while it may sound impossible, unscientific or suspicious to many people, like many of the "miracles" one sees in the Bible, I have had the experience of people telling me dreams about incidents unrelated to their lives, and then reading in the news that these things had subsequently happened, days later.

This uncanny ability is related to the ideas about dreaming and dream states implicit in Bion's concept of O, which he viewed as the domain of the seer or mystic. This mention of occult phenomena is no doubt a significant reason for the widespread controversy about O, which will be examined more fully in Chapters 3 through 6, with reference to mystical and religious states of mind, religious poets and the relationship between religion and science. I will, however, give a brief example below of a prophetic dream, and say something about my experience in interpreting such dreams.

Prophetic dreams and personal dreams

Prophetic dreams are far less common than more personally or emotionally motivated dreams, and far more difficult to identify. I have found by now that I can almost always intuit and interpret the symbolic aspects of the patient's dream by the end of a session, but this is not always the case with a prophetic dream. This is one way that I began to recognize the difference, because, as in the example below, a prophetic dream may strangely fail to evoke any clear ideas in me, in part because prophetic dreams often evoke fewer, or no, associations from the patient, as it is not only about that person's life. This is not to say, however, that such dreams do not also carry personal and emotional meanings that reveal something about the patient's psyche as well. In fact, the presence of these kinds of dreams usually reflects some experiences of the patient's severe early emotional trauma. The dreams of these highly intuitive patients do sometimes foretell distant or future events that would be logically impossible for the person to know about, since they have not yet happened. Mona, one particularly intuitive woman, told me this dream.

> A young boy with an accent was dolefully singing [the patient sings a sweet and simple tune], "Where are the reindeer, where have they gone? Where are the reindeer?

That was all the patient said. She had no associations to reindeer, or to the little boy, or his accent, which sounded vaguely British as she sang the boy's song. I felt there wasn't much I could say without any associations, which was unusual for me when working with dreams. I commented generally on the deep sadness of this little boy's song, a feeling this woman had experienced regularly growing up with an angry father and an overwhelmed, emotionally detached mother, from whom she was temporarily separated at birth due to complications at the birth, but could not say much more. Three days later, however, I read an article in the newspaper saying that approximately 350 reindeer in Norway had been huddled closely together for warmth in a thunderstorm, and when one reindeer was struck by lightning, all 350 of them died. It was reported to have occurred the day before, at least two days *after* Mona's dream. She too had seen this in the news.

As mentioned above, even a prophetic dream bears the stamp of the dreamer's psyche and emotional life, and it is certainly so in this case. Because of her trauma of early separation and deep neglect, Mona was often unconsciously driven to search the world for traumas, as if she were still that neonatal infant searching to find her absent mother. We had seen in many sessions over the years, that all her life, Mona was impelled, psychically, to hunt down and "visit" these worldwide disasters. I saw this as a sort of deeply primitive, unconscious version of a repetition compulsion by which, over and over again, she replayed that early terror. When I first interpreted her need to find her absent mother after birth, she described her experience as "scanning the Universe," which I interpreted as her desperate terror, and her need to locate her mother following her birth. Since then, and in various different ways, she has unconsciously sought out international disasters, devastating earthquakes and tsunamis, days before they occurred, revisiting the devastation of those early weeks of separation from her mother, and not knowing where she, or her mother, was. She manages, in a way I cannot begin to explain, to defy the boundaries of time and space, as she is, again unconsciously, led to events of equally tragic intensity as her early terror.

It became easier to recognize a prophetic dream once I saw that they are often without many associations from the patient, especially if it is a patient who generally has associations. But these dreams are not created only of the dreamer's personal symbols, nor of their early proto-mental non-memories of an event one could not remember. The terror, however, is still clearly alive in Mona. Perhaps the visitations to these tragic events manage to reproduce an experience of those early unremembered "memories," of which she is "reminded" when she senses, somewhere in the world, an explosive energy commensurate with the internal explosion her nervous system must have endured decades ago.

I can imagine that someone reading this might not believe it could happen, but having experienced it in her myself, it is quite real. And so, while this defies logic, this is the territory described in Bion's concept of O, a realm that transcends our finite logical minds and reaches into depths that we cannot even imagine.

I have written about this in relation to Ferenczi's idea concerning occult phenomena in infants who had suffered neglect or abuse at the hands of their mothers (cf. Reiner, 2017, pp. 131–148). Ferenczi hypothesized that infants who experienced severe early emotional trauma, essentially removed themselves psychically from the mother, to a "place" far away, among the stars, which he called "the astra." In an attempt to escape the pain of that early relationship, such children sought a sense of safety and wisdom from the larger universe that was lacking in the maternal relationship (Ferenczi, 1932, pp. 80-82, and pp. 206–207). He referred to these children as "wise babies," because they seemed to receive knowledge that afforded them clairvoyant and telepathic capacities. At the same time, however, they also unknowingly suffered from dissociative states that Ferenczi associated with a fragmentation, or "atomization" of the self (Ferenczi, 1932, pp. 206–207).

We see something like these dynamics in Joseph's story in the Bible, although his severe trauma was not in infancy. The trauma was undeniable, however, for as his father's favorite, he had been the object of morbid jealousy from his brothers, who plotted to kill him, but instead tossed him down an empty well, and later sold him to the Ishmaelites. (Genesis 37–50) Joseph had earlier foreseen these betrayals in a dream, and long before he became the interpreter of dreams who rose to great-ness in Egypt, he also foresaw his brothers and father bowing to him in another dream, an idea for which his father scolded him. While his experience may not exactly follow that of Ferenczi's "wise babies," it is still the story of an especially sensitive child for whom lack of understanding, betrayal, abuse, and suffering may have fueled these breaches in mental boundaries that gave rise to great intuitive gifts, like Mona's forays into the Universe. I have written about several such trau-matized children who also exhibit this kind of gift (Reiner, 2004, 2016).

As in Neruda's poem, there have always been questions about the source of dreams. Pharaoh and Joseph saw them as messages from God, for when Pharaoh announces that no one had so far been able to interpret his dream, he expresses his hope that Joseph will be able to do so. Joseph replies, "I do not count. It is God who will give Pharaoh a favorable answer" (Genesis 41:17). Then, after he hears Pharaoh's dream, Joseph says, "God has revealed to Pharaoh what he is going to do" (Genesis 41: 25–26). It is God who is responsible for the events that will occur. While I, along with most psychoanalysts, would not see it that way, at least not in the sense of a traditional, anthropomorphic God responsible for the events of man-kind, but rather as a belief in another form of mental activity determined, not by the logical brain, but rather through access to a metaphysical, mystical reality beyond our finite awareness. Bion's concept of O is a version of that God, which he calls the "Godhead," in order to differentiate it from that reified anthropomorphic God. Again, we cannot know what Joseph (if indeed there was a "Joseph") had in mind when he attributed his interpretations to "God," for religious institutions and tradi-tion have fairly typically transformed the mystical notion of God into that reified, omnipotent Being.

The difference is contained in the Gnostic Gospels, which were written at roughly the same time as the Christian Gospels, but did not speak of Jesus as a God, as it was suggested, or interpreted to mean, in the Christian Gospels. Rather, Jesus was presented as a teacher of divine knowledge that each fol-lower had the responsibility to learn for themselves (Pagels, 1989). This Gnostic "God" is closer to what Bion meant by the Godhead, where O is a symbol of that divine knowledge that each person must learn. It is distinct from the omnipotent, punishing or rewarding God of the Old Testament, and from the stereotypical Christian version of a loving Jesus as God in the New Testament. The Godhead reflects the religious *feeling of awe* before those higher truths, rather than an awesome power of an external God to whom one must pledge one faith, and one's fate. It is the difference between a symbol and a symbolic equation, where Christ does not represent the divine knowledge, but is felt to be God, per se (Segal, 1981), a God that bestows his power on his subjects. The real symbol of divine knowledge implies a higher sense of responsibility for one's fate, determined by one's own morality. This higher conscience represents the development of an inner moral sense, independent of the blessings or condemnation of an external God.

This basic differentiation between the religious, reified God and the divine knowledge of the Godhead will be fully discussed in Chapter 3 on O, through poems by Rumi, Hafiz and others. It is a relationship with one's own internal dream-poems of depth, complexity and meaning.

Poetry in a changing world

The diminished importance of poetry, an art form previously so admired, may in part reflect the diminished importance of truth that permeates modern society and politics. Without truth there is no dependable sense of reality, under which conditions the mind cannot continue to exist and grow. This is evident to us in psychotic states and serious mental illness, but is so at every level of mental life, for it is a destruction of both the container and the contents of the mind. Bion described truth as nourishment for the mind, while lies and untruths are toxic to its health and growth.

> Whatever is falsely employed as a substitute for the real, is transformed thereby into a poison for the mind.
>
> (Bion, 1992, p. 299)

The mind's capacity for truth requires upkeep. Bion's theories of thinking are based on the idea that the development of the mind does not occur automatically, for while we human beings are born with the *potential* for a mind, the capacity to think, according to Bion (1962, 1963), must be developed under certain conditions in the relationship with the mother's mind. The mother's mind, in particular, her capacity for reverie, serves as a container for the infant's feelings, which the infant is then in a position to process and digest. Without these conditions, the infant's potential mind often takes a different path *away from truth of his or her feelings, a path of unconscious lies that cannot process its inherent potential capacity to feel and think.* And yet our individual mental survival, and the survival of humanity, depend upon the development of our minds. Looking around at the place to which truth has devolved, we are face with an essential conflict about the importance of truth, and the importance of having a mind to perceive it.

This conflict may be completely unconscious. It is easy to be led astray by the false belief that as human beings we have already achieved these basic mental capacities, when in fact, after approximately a mere 7,000 years of civilization, humankind is very much at the beginning of this daunting but worthwhile journey. Much of Bion's work aimed at reminding us of how far we have to go to evolve into our human potential, or at least to begin to evolve toward the knowledge of the kind of mind we are inherently programmed to develop.

On a more positive note, Bion (1979) writes in his fictionalized autobiography, *The Dawn of Oblivion,*

> Truth is robust; 'facts' cannot be killed even if we do not know what they are. The fragile human respect for truth cannot be as easily disposed of as often appears.
>
> (Bion, 1979, p. 499)

The health of our minds depends upon the Truth. We need Truth, despite the fact that Truth does not need us to think it. It will still be true, in other words, whether or not we think it.

While there are many people who are still interested in thinking, the trend in the United States, and so many countries, is toward an inability to agree, even on the truth of the simplest facts, let alone the nuances of philosophical thought that are involved in psychoanalytic work, and the development of the mind. The purpose of poetry has obviously changed in a world filled increasingly with ubiquitous modes of entertainment and media that often distract, rather than develop, our minds. Poetry's purpose may once have been to help us remember important historical events, like wars, to understand and give meaning to the experiences that shape people's sense of who they are. By now, with various types of media at our fingertips every day, and often *all* day, we have so many ways to record history, with much less effort than slogging through the often heavy tomes of poetry and literature. Is it technology that has seduced us away from poetry, and from our connection to the deeper parts of our personalities? Is it laziness? A desire for certainty? Is it a hatred of reality itself or our reluctance to challenge our hubris, omnipotence, and arrogance, our defenses, in other words, against the awareness of our own ignorance and limitations? Or is it the hatred of truth itself, which may best be reached through contemplative states, easily drowned out by the distractions? It is undoubtedly easier to pretend we understand the meaning of our lives than it is actually to understand it.

Somewhere on the border between the inner and outer worlds, that capacity for meditative silence provides an opportunity to integrate those two worlds, which is a necessary part of how artists transform reality into works of art, as well as how viewers and readers appreciate them. And according to Bion it is the same meditative silence he represented by O.

The plight of the poet is not dissimilar to that of the contemporary psychoanalyst, as both have grown increasingly unpopular to the masses, probably *because* both are contemplative examinations of the hidden metaphysical worlds that not only live within us, but also, in an essential way, *are* us. While some people continue to appreciate poetry, it inhabits a very small and usually less than lucrative niche in the publishing world, and in the hearts of many people throughout the modern world. But for many others, vis-á-vis depth poetry, or psychoanalysis, the question seems to be, "Why go there if we don't have to?" The truth is we don't all have to go to those deeper places. And from the perspective of what Winnicott (1960) called the False Self, whose job, as he put it, "is to organize the suicide [of the True Self]" (p. 143), it may be hard to find a reason to uncover the painful, forgotten emotions of one's long-lost True Self. Mothers who could not receive the true reality of their infants' emotional or existential selves, often leave their children feeling that the buried or unborn inner self is best left unborn. It feels, at best, to be of no importance, and at worst, the repository of intolerably painful feelings that constantly threaten to emerge and overthrow their uneasy peace. However, it may become necessary to go there if something happens that puts one in touch with the fact that one feels lost, or does not really know if one exists. At that point, one may be compelled to find out the truth, despite the many reasons *not* to find out, namely the fear and hatred of truth. Á propos of this resistance to truth in psychoanalytic work. Bion wrote:

I have rarely failed to experience hatred of analysis, and its reciprocal, sexualization of psychoanalysis… The human animal has not ceased to be persecuted by his mind and the thoughts usually associated with it… Therefore, I do not expect any psycho-analysis properly done to escape the odium inseparable from the mind.

(Bion, 1970, p. 126)

It is our ignorance and fear of the unknown that causes such intense aversions to reality and truth. In fact, even the esteemed 20th century poet, Marianne Moore, was not immune to it. In her poem entitled, "Poetry," she wrote:
I, too, dislike it: there are things that are important beyond all this fiddle.

Reading it, however, with a perfect contempt for it, one discovers in it after all, a place for the genuine.

(Moore, 1921, p. 457)

The widespread discomfort, or even antipathy to poetry, seems to derive from a similar place as the resistance Bion describes in psychoanalysis, a resistance to the profound mystery of our own minds. Obviously, this is not the whole picture, for despite the challenges posed by both poetry and psychoanalysis, both do also "provide a place for the genuine," for which many people retain a burning need. William Carlos Williams similarly wrote:

It is difficult
to get the news from poems
yet men die miserably every day
for lack of what is found there.
       (Williams, pp. 150–151)

This kind of "news," and this "place for the genuine," are also sorely needed. Our minds, even our lives, may depend upon it. I know this from experience. Decades ago, my own sense of self was deeply challenged, which was alarming enough to compel me to try to find out the truth. This happily coincided with the time Bion lived and worked in Los Angeles, and he, along with some of his analysands, were instrumental in my learning what I then knew I needed to learn. I was richly rewarded for my efforts, for it was after this that I began painting and writing poetry, short stories, plays, children's books and psychoanalytic books and papers. I found my need to think about and express deep feelings. While my appreciation for poetry grew enormously, I am by no means well-versed (no pun intended) in all kinds of poetry. Nor am I a poetry snob, and I do find it refreshing to hear poets like Moore, and analysts like Bion, admit how rigorous and perplexing it can be.

Bion was not afraid to admit how much one can hate psychoanalysis, because it *is* such a challenge for both patients and psychoanalysts, but that grappling with this challenge helps our minds to grow, which provides an endlessly fascinating source of authentic meaning, growth and connection to ourselves and others. One might also eventually recognize that it is an honor to help others to find meaning, health and beauty in their lives.

References

Bion, W. R. (1962). *Learning from Experience*. New York: Basic Books.

Bion, W. R. (1963). *Elements of Psychoanalysis*. New York: Basic Books.

Bion, W. R. (1965). *Transformations*. London: William Heinemann. In *Seven Servants* (pp. 1–183). New York: Jason Aronson, 1977.

Bion, W. R. (1970). *Attention and Interpretation*. London: Karnac.

Bion, W. R. (1978). *Private Seminar*. Bion's Home in Brentwood, California.

Bion, W. R. (1979). The dawn of oblivion. In *Memoir of the Future, Book 3* (pp. 427–578). London: Karnac, 1991.

Bion, W. R. (1992). *Cogitations*. London: Karnac.

Exodus. In A. Jones, (Ed.). *The Jerusalem Bible*. New York: Doubleday & Co.

Ferenczi, S. (1932). *The Clinical Diary of Sándor Ferenczi.* In J. Dupont (Ed.), M. Balint; N. Z. Jackson (Trans.).. Cambridge, MA: Harvard University Press, 1995.

Freud, E. (Ed.) (1960). *The Letters of Sigmund Freud, 1873–1939*. New York, Basic Books.

Freud, S. (1900). Chapter VII, The Psychology of the Dream-Processes: The primary and secondary processes--repression. In *The Interpretation of Dreams, Second Part, Standard Edition*, 5 (pp. 588–609). London: Hogarth Press, 1958.

Freud, S. (1937). *Analysis Terminable of Interminable, Standard Edition*, 23 (pp. 216–253). London: Hogarth Press.

Grotstein, J. S. (2000). *Who is the Dreamer Who Dreams the Dream?* Hillsdale, NJ: The Analytic Press.

Leopardi, G. (1826). A letter to Francesco Puccinotti, June 5, 1826. In E. Grennan (Trans.). *Leopardi, Selected Poems,* (Frontispiece). Princeton, NJ: Princeton University Press, 1997.

Moore, M. (1921). Poetry. In R. Ellman; R. O'Clair (Eds.). *The Norton Anthology of Modern Poetry, Second Edition* (pp. 454–459). New York, W. W. Norton & Company, 1973.

Neruda, P. (2003). The Sea. In A. Reid (Trans.). *Neruda: on the Blue Shore of Silence (Poems of the Sea), Estate of Pablo Neruda*. New York: HarperCollins Publishers, 2003.

Pagels, E. (1989). *The Gnostic Gospels*. New York, Vintage Books.

Plato. (37 B.C.E.). Ion. In E. Hamilton; H. Cairns (Eds.), L. Cooper (Trans.). *Plato: Collected Dialogues* (pp. 215–228). Bollingen Series LXXI. Princeton, NJ: Princeton University Press, 1961.

Reiner, A. (2004). Psychic phenomena and early emotional life. *Journal of Analytical Psychology*, 49: 313–336.

Reiner, A. (2008). The language of the unconscious: Poetry and psychoanalysis. *The Psychoanalytic Review*, 95: 4.

Reiner, A. (2012). Bion and Being: Passion and the Creative Mind. London: Karnac.

Reiner, A. (2017). Ferenczi's 'astra' and Bion's 'O': A clinical perspective. In A. Reiner (Ed.). *Of Things Invisible to Mortal Sight: Celebrating the Work of James S. Grotstein* (pp. 131–148). London: Karnac, 2017.

Rumi. (1981). The ruins of the heart. In E. Helminski (Trans.) (pp. 36–38). Putney, VT: Threshold Books.

Segal, H. (1981). Notes on symbol formation. In *The Work of Hannah Segal: A Kleinian Approach to Clinical Practice* (pp. 49–68). New York: Jason Aronson.

Tromly, F. (1968). *Introduction to Milton's Paradise Lost and Paradise Regained*. Clinton, MA: Airmont Publishing Company.

Welles, O., Bogdanovich, P., & Rosenbaum, J. (Eds.). (1998). *This is Orson Welles*. New York: Da Capo Press.

Williams, W. C. (1949). Asphodel, that greeny flower, Book I. In *William Carlos Williams Selected Poems* (pp. 142–151). New York: New Directions Publishing Co.

Winnicott, D. W. (1960). Ego distortion in terms of the true and false self. In *Maturational Processes and the Facilitating Environment* (pp. 140–152). London, New York: Karnac, 1965.

Chapter 2

The search for truth

The Naked I

Take off your dark glasses,
take off your mother's glasses,
your father's glasses,
your blind theories of everything you know—
what the hell, take off your clothes.
From bare trees green leaves will fall into your hand,
and you will read them like a gypsy
with crystal vision.
All over town you'll see
nothing but naked children—
bankers, lawyers, doctors
who otherwise appear so permanently dressed
will show you their soft bellies
and secret scars.
Teacher's strip their curricula,
instructing children
only to keep their eyes naked,
to see for the first time
what they've always known.

(Reiner, 1994, p. 10)[1]

With O, Bion is talking about instinctual knowledge, *a priori* knowledge of a primordial or proto-mental mind that exists from birth or before. Like the end of the poem above, these are things we know but cannot remember, for this "knowledge" is at the same time unknown and unthinkable to the infant who has not yet developed a mind able to think. It is the one instance that I know of, in which Bion directly compared his ideas to Jung's. In a lecture Bion gave in Los Angeles, an audience member asked if Bion's discussion of a "primordial mind" was similar to Jung's archetypes, and he replied:

DOI: 10.4324/9781003470953-3

I think [Jung] was probably talking about the same thing. There exists some fundamental mind, something that remains unaltered in us all.

(Bion, 1978a, p. 4)

Jung's collective unconscious seemed to reflect what Bion also referred to as a proto-mental system that exists in the infant before birth. It is well-known that the consequential differences between Jung and Freud ultimately proved destructive to their partnership, and that some aspects of a mystical perspective were a significant part of their rift. In the Jungian community over the last several decades, there has been a steadily growing interest in Bion's work because of these similarities, and despite the differences that still exist between Bion's Psychoanalytic perspective and the Analytic Psychology of Jung's perspective. The Society of Analytical Psychology in London and Wales describes what they call a "Third Modality" which aims at sharing the knowledge of both groups. While I cannot know what this will ultimately yield, they have an upcoming conference in 2025 called, "BION MEETS JUNG: A Third Modality," based on efforts to work toward sharing their ideas. In the vastness and ambiguity of human mental life, too much certainty about one's own truths can breed unnecessary hostility that obstructs new ideas.

Humor

The following quote has been variously attributed to George Bernard Shaw, Oscar Wilde, and Richard Pryor, among others.

If you want to tell people the truth, make them laugh. Otherwise they will kill you.

We can safely rule out Richard Pryor as the original source of this statement, since he had prefaced it with, "As someone once said…" Despite the controversy about who actually said it, the statement suggests a fear and perceived danger of truth, and the need to sugarcoat it, in this case with humor. It is relevant to the challenges inherent in delivering the truth to someone, as psychoanalysts must do every day, and it speaks to a question Bion posed in a clinical seminar I had with him in 1977. After listening to the case material that was presented, Bion asked the group, "How can we get the interpretation to the right address?" (Bion, 1977). While his question was enigmatic, it reflected the fact that if we have a truth to share, how can we make sure that the patient can hear it? Interpretation, in other words, is more than just being able to say something but determining whether it can penetrate to the deep level of a patient's mind that can actually hear what we say.

Bion's (1962) idea of the "selected fact" addressed this challenge clinically, for it deals with our need to find the relevant aspect of a session that has the power and specificity to resonate with the patient. It is a scientific perspective on mental truths for which we need evidence within the session that validates our idea, just as scientists need evidence to prove the truths of their theories in the physical world. It is difficult to do psychoanalytically, since that relevant "selected fact" is often embedded within the overwhelming amount of stimuli of the patient's words, feelings, associations, body language, and dreams. It depends on the challenge of how to find the central truth in a session, O, and the awareness of how the patient receives it.

Psychoanalysts regularly confront patients with emotional truths that may have been unconscious for decades, and which are often met with some form of resistance, sometimes of an emotionally violent nature. Bion (1965) wrote, "Resistance operates because it is feared that reality is imminent" (p. 147). From this perspective, fear of the unconscious is not engendered only by repressed impulses or unwanted thoughts, rather it is reality itself that people find fearsome. In Bion's terms, resistance is a resistance to O, a resistance to getting in touch with a deeper level of "ultimate reality," "absolute truth," and a sense of the infinite. Why we are so frightened of reality is a complex question at the heart of psychoanalytic work, namely the nature of the mind itself, particularly an infinite and unknowable mind that is beyond our awareness and control. As Bion also said:

> The development of the mind has been a frightful nuisance, and has caused an awful lot of trouble. I think we are still frightened of it.
>
> (Bion, 1978b, p. 53)

In Bion's lexicon, "mind" is a term he used as synonymous with "self," "character," or "personality" – the essence or spirit of one's being – rather than the common usage of "mind" that more narrowly suggests intelligence or intellect. Because our own minds or personalities or selves are unknown to us, we are faced with the uncertain challenge of how to know who we are, and how to trust what we consciously believe to be reality. Bion's concept of O focuses on that ultimately unknowable reality beyond our sense-based knowledge of the world, a deeper level of awareness that makes us mysteries, even to ourselves.

This unknowable internal reality is seemingly easy to ignore since it cannot be seen or heard or otherwise sensually detected, but it does not disappear. The powerful energy of those disregarded feelings and thoughts eventually makes itself known to us through anxiety or depression, or "…the thousand natural shocks that flesh is heir to" (Hamlet, Shakespeare, 1600, Act III, sc.i, p. 93, lines 62–63). The resistance to this level of truth was evident in the negative reactions that Bion's ideas often evoked, as if he were the personification of the unknown truths about which people preferred not to know.

O – scientific and mystical truth

Many analysts are interested in O, that essence of absolute truth, but find the meaning of this elusive, metaphysical idea frustrating and out of reach. It is unclear why some people react to this kind of frustration with antipathy and depreciation, while others may react with curiosity and a desire to find a way to understand it. The latter was my experience when I went to hear Bion speak throughout the 1970s, for as a young therapist in my mid-twenties, I certainly did not grasp the meaning and implications of O, or many other things of which he spoke. I can only now attribute my reaction to my sense that what he said "rang true," although what it "rang" in me was no doubt a very distant bell. Whatever the source of my interest, I felt that there was something profoundly true in what he was saying, despite my own lack of understanding. I think that distant bell was an example of Bion's idea of "thoughts without a thinker," the idea that these absolute truths exist whether or not we are able to think them. And so while I was clearly unable to think it, it was conceivably (or pre-conceptually), a thought that might someday be "thinkable," for the sense I had was that Bion, for one, was already thinking it.

As we might deduce from the idea quoted above about humor being a sort of "spoonful of sugar" that could make the "medicine" of truth more palatable, and it reflect the fact that what matters is not only *what* one says but *how* one says it. Both the form and the content create the message, and humor is really another form of art that may be used in poems or literature. It is certainly present in visual art as well, for instance, in some surrealist art, like the ironic painting by Magritte depicting a pipe, beneath which the words painted read, "*Ce n'est pas une pipe*" ("This is not a pipe"). Humor can turn reality on its head, a way of temporarily standing our logic on its head, which can let in a new or conflicting idea.

Truth and humor

Humorists and comedians widely agree that for something to be genuinely funny, it must be based in truth. When we recognize the foibles in ourselves being played out in others, we laugh, relieved to see our common humanity being shared, and being able to laugh at what may otherwise feel painful, shameful, embarrassing, or lonely. Sharing a laugh makes us feel part of a community, which makes humor an irresistible tool, and used in that way, it may at that moment help to get the unpleasant truth to the "right address." One may find oneself laughing, in spite of oneself, as pain is transformed into joy.

Samuel Beckett was a master of dark comedy. This is the first line in *Murphy*, one of Becket's first novels.

> The sun shone, having no alternative, on the nothing new. Murphy sat out of it, as though he were free…
>
> (Beckett, 1957, p. 1)

In these two simple lines, one senses helplessness and enduring hopelessness, lightened by humor. Humor is a form of alchemy, which can transform existential dread and despair into something lighter, even pleasurable. While it does not solve the problem, it sheds light on the darkness, provides another perspective on the experience that temporarily mitigates the pain. Again, truth is a necessity in humor, and by putting something painful into words, saying it out loud, perhaps after having been hidden for so long, it shines that light on the darkness, providing a sense of freedom, that nothing is so bad that it cannot be known.

Like Beckett, Bion had a dry sense of humor, which he was not averse to using in analytic work. When one patient, questioning his interpretation, asked Bion, "Are you being sarcastic?" Bion thought for a moment, then said, "If not… why not?" In his ironic way, he was asking why sarcasm, irony, or humor should be off limits? I experienced another example of his wry humor after I had read in a biography of Beckett that Bion had been Beckett's therapist at the Tavistock Clinic in 1934, after Beckett suffered a breakdown (Bair, 1978, p. 176). I asked Bion about this after a lecture in Los Angeles, and he paused and said, "Yes, I don't believe I helped him very much." Again, this was funny because it was so disarmingly truthful, if not perhaps overly humble.

Like all things human, humor has its place in psychoanalysis, although analysts do not typically use humor in what are often such serious matters of mental life, where the aim is to feel the depth of the pain, not mitigate it. However, as above, there are exceptions to this, if and when the moment is right, and if the person has a sense of humor, something which cannot simply be assumed. But humor is a human characteristic, and so to banish it altogether is not realistic. Since O is the absolute truth that exists between patient and analyst in that moment, that truth may include humor, or really anything else, and as long as it is not destructive to either participant, nothing human should be forbidden.

We know, of course, that like anything pleasurable, laughter can be used as a defense against painful realities, and even in the form of psychotic, manic defenses, for instance, where truth or reality becomes unreachable. But humor is not only for the evasion of difficult truths, any more than the pleasures of art or poetry are simply evasions of the truth, for they are also helpful in revealing a deeper understanding of painful truths that can make emotional pain more tolerable without evading it. The Arts, in any form, can help in making otherwise painful truths more palatable. As Nietzsche (1888) put it, "We possess Art lest we perish of truth" (p. 435, section 822).

Despite the transformations of painful realities through the Arts, we have to face the fact that many people are more likely to kill off their own feelings, or psychically "kill" the truth, or the analyst, emotionally at least, for being the bearer of bad news. While there are certainly those who more readily embrace the truth, it is hard to deny that many people are not particularly endowed with a great love of truth. In many cases, people deprived of truth in their early lives may not know quite what to do with it, and must be helped to develop a taste for truth. Emily Dickinson speaks to a similar idea about the fear and perceived danger of truth, and the dangers of poetry as conveyers of truth.

Tell all the Truth but tell it slant,
Success in Circuit lies,
Too bright for our infirm Delight
The Truth's superb surprise

As Lightning to the Children eased
With explanations kind
The Truth must dazzle gradually
Or every man be blind.
            (Dickinson, 1945, p. 53)

Absence of truth is itself a kind of blindness, of which one may be completely una-ware. But the last two lines reflect the delicacy of our capacity to tolerate truth, for hearing it too soon or conveyed too clumsily can instill fear that leads one to be fur-ther blinded by the truth. Dickinson's poem implies the possibility of poetry to con-vey painful truths, but only if one "tells it slant," for it is the artistry that can help to make it more tolerable to think about. Part of that artistry is the ability to use symbols that helps the truth to enter the mind at a different level, like a dream, and so poetry's idiosyncratic form of language – symbolic, metaphorical, and associative – is itself a way of using words in a way that can "tell it slant." It is the same method, men-tioned above (Foreword), that Christ made use of parables – metaphorical, symbolic representations better suited to express the elusive matters of the spirit. It is certainly applicable to psychoanalysis as well, in the same need to express unconscious inner realities unavailable to sensory data. In making interpretations, the analyst has to be careful to express something that is evident in the current material, which the patient is ready to hear, or the individual may not be able to receive it. Interpretations that are repetitions of already known theories, that are not timely or cogent, may fall flat, and so analysts also attempt to, "Tell all the Truth but tell it slant." In work-ing with dreams, the psychoanalyst does this by using the "poetry" of the patient's own dreams. This helps the analyst to present the patient's own symbols that may speak directly to something more essential, and unconscious, than one's logically remembered theories. As in poetry, the symbols and metaphors in dreams, as well as the symbols gleaned through the waking dreams and inadvertently revealed through patients' associations, are ways the analyst can "tell it slant" as well.

The language of dreams uses those same tools of poetry – symbols, metaphors, images, parables – to address truths that cannot be expressed in strictly logical lan-guage. Our ordinary, rational use of language is adequate in expressing experiences gained through the physical world of our senses, and while this may allow us to tell the patient something of what we have learned about him, telling it "slant" allows us to *show* the individual something through his or her own emotional experience embedded in the metaphorical and symbolic language of the dream. Although none of us easily understands the "poetry" of our own dreams, they do naturally employ Dickinson's suggestion to "tell it slant."

Clinical vignette

To give a simple clinical example, "Eric" is a novelist who came for treatment for writer's block. In the first session he explained, "I keep trying to write, but whatever I'm working on, I pick it up, and then I put it down and just can't get back to it. It's frustrating." He then spoke about growing up with four siblings and a single mother who was overwhelmed and depressed, and he often felt desperate for her attention. He tried different ways to get close to his mother, often as her special helper.

In this session, I could feel his vulnerability, but could not make sense of the underlying meaning of what he was saying. After a while, a simple poetic figure of speech caught my attention, and like Bion's idea of finding the selected fact, it reveals what is relevant and essential in a session about the patient's state of mind. I kept hearing in my mind his statement about his writing dilemma, "I pick it up and then I put it down." This simple idea seemed to me to be the point of the session, a kind of double entendre that in a way was "telling it slant." On a rational level he was talking about *physically* putting down the work, unable to work anymore, but what I heard included the meaning of having been "put down" or devalued, like being *emotionally* dropped from his mother's distracted mind, which he now does to himself each time he tries to write. On this level he is essentially dropping himself, for in "putting his work down," he is also putting *himself* down," a harsh judgment of both himself and his work as bad. Since his mother was not available to hear him, the unconscious conclusion that Eric seemed to reach as a child, was that he was unworthy of being heard, and unworthy of having his own voice. His writing block reflects this old trauma of having no one listening, and so why speak at all, or in this case, why write?

This is the poetry of his dreaming mind that is still fighting to be heard, and understood, without knowing what needs to be said or heard. The internal voice that puts him down was his infantile interpretation of his mother's judgment of him as unworthy to be heard, a punishing internal voice, that we would call a primitive superego, that just keeps "putting him down." With this simple phrase, that punishing superego was revealed in this very first session, and it uncovered a part of him that has always judged him for not being good enough to warrant his mother's love.

Despite the perceived dangers of truth, the psychoanalyst's job is to face these difficult or unknown truths, but even in analysis, we have to do it "slant." This does not imply a distortion of the truth, but rather a way of hearing and communicating the truth from a perspective that reveals its deeper meaning.

Union of form and content

The essential idea of the selected fact in the session is as elusive as the meaning of a poem.

> The subject of a poem is as foreign to it and as important, as his name is to a man.
>
> (Valéry, 1950, p. 148)

Even the poem, Valéry suggests, does not seem to know what it is about, for its meaning derives from the nonsensual metaphysical world. It is not the poet's logical mind that creates the poem, for it is born of an often elusive and intense *feeling* that takes over the more prosaic, waking mind, much as a dream takes over the sleeping mind. The poem is created directly by the feeling itself, which then works with the waking mind in a mysterious dance. It may feel like an autochthonous birth, as if it is giving birth to itself, but it does depend on some kind of communication with the logical waking mind.

Valéry alludes to a capacity of poetry to bring harmony between inner and outer life, through a unity between form and content. Both the form and content of the poem are created in the energy of that dream-like self, not by a rational mind that sets out to impose a specific subject or idea, and to fit that idea into an already determined form. These poems arrive like a dream, and like the creator of the dream who is asleep, the poet, although technically awake, receives the energy of that intuitive and emotional dreaming mind which allows the poem to speak in its idiosyncratic language. This waking-dream state that Bion called O creates the poem, just as the interpretation is given its shape by a similar communion between the thinking and feeling mind.

Valéry expresses this in his comparison of that elusive subject of a poem and the illusory nature of a man's name. While one's name may seem to be one's identity, and so of great importance, ontologically speaking, one's name *is not who one really is*, but just a *symbol* of who one is. In the end it is a word, while the spirit or mind or self is a much more complex expression of one's self that may be both unknowable and inexpressible. In a sense, as Shakespeare said over 400 years earlier, one needs to *forget* who one is, in order to *be* who one is. Here, Juliet says to Romeo about their feuding families:

> *Tis but thy name that is my enemy.*
> *Thou art thyself, though not a Montague.*
> *What's Montague? It is nor hand, nor foot,*
> *Nor arm, nor face, nor any other part*
> *Belonging to a man. O, be some other name!*
> *What's in a name? That which we call a rose*
> *By any other name would smell as sweet.*
> *So Romeo would, were he not Romeo called,*
> *Retain that dear perfection which he owes*
> *Without that title. Romeo, doff thy name;*
> *And for that name, which is no part of thee,*
> *Take all myself.*
> (Shakespeare, 1591, pp. 29–30)

Romeo replies:

> I take thee at thy word.
> Call me love, and I'll be new baptised;
> Henceforth I never will be Romeo.
> (Shakespeare, 1591, p. 30)

The word or name is not the essence of a thing, which, like O, the unknown and unknowable thing-in-itself, cannot be known, even if it is oneself. Likewise, the subject or content of the poem may also be somehow hidden within or behind the words, in a way that one may be able to feel, but cannot really know. Valéry writes:

> Thought is hidden in verse like the nutritive virtue in fruit... one perceives only pleasure but one receives substance.
>
> (Valéry, 1950, pp. 147–148)

One may not know what one has actually received from the experience of a poem. Unlike poetry, of course, the aim of psychoanalysis is not to give pleasure or to entertain. As Bion (1970) stated, the practice of psychoanalysis is often hated, both by the patient and the analyst, in part because of the emotional turmoil it provokes. Nevertheless, in its role of imparting truth, both parties can derive a certain kind of pleasure, because of the nutritive value in truth, as a corollary of mental growth and consciousness. These reflect the inherent human potential that we are instinctually driven to fulfill, and so despite the pain it may cause, both patient and analyst receive this nutritive value. At that fundamental instinctual level, whether through analysis or poetry or any other means, the "taste" of truth can nourish the mind, by capturing a moment of consciousness and mental life from the jaws of mental darkness.

It is difficult for words of logic themselves to convey the meaning of the inherently complex and mysterious union of the inner and outer self. Like Bion's idea of binocular vision, whereby the unconscious function of dreaming must work together with consciousness for a bimodal, binary perspective (Bion, 1962, p. 54), that union is possible when inner and outer selves can work together to give the poet an experience of unity. The poem, then, may bear the stamp of that unity, which can be imparted to those who read it. Whether for the poet, artist, or psychoanalyst, the aim of the work is to develop that sense of unity within the mind, that binocularity, that can then be shared with the patient.

Creativity and Bion's concept of 'O'

A lot of attention will be given in subsequent chapters, to examining the waking-dream state of 'O', both as it relates to the analyst's capacity to work with the unconscious, and in how this state of mind facilitates the creative process of anyone engaged in creative work – poets, artists, writers, philosophers, and musicians. It should be clear from what has already been said that Bion recognized the importance of artistic expression as a sort of coordinate language and coordinate state of mind to the language of logic and reason in psychoanalytic work. Here he highlights the elusive nature of truth.

> I was compelled to seek asylum in fiction. Disguised as fiction, the truth occasionally slipped through.
>
> (Bion, 1991, p. 302)

This statement is aptly attributed to a character in Bion's fictionalized autobiography, *The Past Presented*, which consists largely of conversations between his many inner voices, each representing different aspects of his personality and experiences. It is also fitting that the fictionalized character who makes this statement in the book is the voice of "P.A." – representing Bion's Psychoanalyst-self, someone who recognizes the need to use language in the ways that artists do in order to express these deeper truths of mental life. Freud also acknowledged the fact that poets and artists are well-situated, or better-situated, to understand these profound states. In a letter to the author, Roman Rolland, he writes:

> It is easier for you [writers] than for us [psychoanalysts] to read the human soul.
> (Freud, 1960, p 389)

This is not meant to suggest that it is the same process in each of these fields, or that psychoanalysis does not provide its own, and necessary, contribution to the apprehension of truth. Rather it is to make the point that it includes a need to understand the mind through intuitive means, much as artists and writers do. It is difficult to express deeper truths of an infinite nature in the language of a finite mind. I think Freud's comment makes the case that Bion's concept of O is a necessary addition to our understanding of what is necessary if we are to understand the depth and complexity of that infinite unconscious mind.

Bion's statement about psychoanalysis

I will end this chapter with what I think is an intriguing statement by Bion. It seems somewhat unsettling at first, but is ultimately a hopeful expression of the importance he saw in exercising these complementary though different mental functions in analytic work.

> It is very important to be aware that you may never be satisfied with your analytic career if you feel that you are restricted to what is narrowly called a 'scientific' approach. You will have to be able to have a chance of feeling that the interpretation you give is a beautiful one, or that you get a beautiful response from the patient. This aesthetic element of beauty makes a very difficult situation tolerable. It is so important to dare to think or feel whatever you do think or feel, never mind how un-scientific it is.
> (Bion, *The Paris Seminar*, p. 211)

After many years, I have felt this often in my appreciation of patients' dreams, a sense of awe, even, in face of the mystery and wisdom of the unconscious, and the courage some people have to open their minds to these dream states beyond their control. They too can then begin to see the sometimes awesome beauty and unity of what their minds create for them to think about, and for us to think about together.

As we will see in subsequent chapters, Bion's idea of a "narrowly" defined scientific approach does not suggest a negative view of science, or the absence of a scientific perspective in psychoanalytic work, rather he describes the need to expand that narrowly defined "'scientific' approach" to include the inner world of the mind as well. His transcendent perspective of O reflects his attempts at facilitating that experience of unification within oneself.

In these efforts, we need to accept the fact that the experience of integration and unity of one's mind is always temporary, but with the knowledge that, with our efforts, it can be revisited again, whether in creating another work of art, or another interpretation that can bring temporary unity to the analyst's and the patient's mind. These moments of unity and authenticity are ways of exercising the potential for truth and beauty that we embody as human beings, and however temporary, as Bion suggests, this helps to make the difficult work of psychoanalysis more tolerable. It is hard to believe that anyone could put up with the pain of analysis if this were not so.

Note

1 This poem was a winner in the 1992 Los Angeles Poetry Festival Contest. Los Angeles: Red Wind Books, 1993, p. 39.

References

Bair, D. (1978). *Samuel Beckett: A Biography*. New York, London: Harcourt Brace Jovanovich.
Beckett, S. (1938/1957). *Murphy*. New York: Grove Press.
Bion, W. R. (1962). *Learning from Experience*. New York: Basic Books.
Bion, W. R. (1965). Transformations. In *Seven Servants* (pp. 1–183). New York: Jason Aronson, 1977.
Bion, W. R. (1970). *Attention and Interpretation*. London: Karnac
Bion, W.R. (1977). Private Clinical Seminar., Bion's home. Los Angeles, CA: Homewood Road.
Bion, W. R. (1978a). *Four Discussion with W. R. Bion*. Perthshire: Cluny Press.
Bion, W. R. (1978b). Seminar 5, 4 July, 1978. In F. Bion (Ed.). *The Tavistock Seminars* (pp. 53–56). London: Karnac, 2005.
Bion, W. R. (1978c). A *Paris Seminar.* 10 July 1978. In C. Mawson (Ed.) *Complete Works of W. R. Bion,* vol. IX (pp. 201–211), London: Karnac, 2014.
Bion, W. R. (1991). The past presented. In *Memoir of the Future, Book Two* (pp. 221–426). London: Karnac.
Dickinson, E. (1945). Tell all the truth… In R. Ellman; R. O'Clair (Eds.). *The Norton Anthology of Modern Poetry, Second Edition*. New York, London: W.W. Norton & Company.
Freud, E. (Ed.) (1960). Letters of Sigmund Freud, *1873–1939*. In T. Stern; J. Stern (Trans.). New York: Basic Books.
Nietzsche, F. (1888). The Will to Power. In W. Kaufmann; R. J. Hollingdale (Trans.). New York: Vintage Books/Random House, 1967.
Reiner, A. (1994). The Naked I. In *The Naked I*. Lancaster, CA: Red Dancefloor Press.
Shakespeare, W. (1591). *Romeo and Juliet*. Act II, sc. 2. In L. B. Wright; V. A. LaMar (Eds.) (pp. 29–30). New York: The Folger Library Shakespeare, Pocket Books (A division of Simon & Shuster), 1959.
Shakespeare, W. (1600). Hamlet. Act III, sc. i. In E. Hubler (Ed.). New York, Toronto: The New American Library, 1963.
Valéry, P. (1950). *Selected Writings of Paul Valéry*. New York: New Directions Publishing Co.

Chapter 3

'O' in mysticism, religion and psychoanalysis

Seasons return, but not to me returns
Day, or the sweet approach of even or morn,
Or sight of vernal bloom, or summer's rose,
Or flocks, or herds, or human face divine;
But cloud instead, and ever-during dark
Surrounds me...
Of nature's works to me expunged and rased,
And wisdom at one entrance, quite shut out.
So much rather thou celestial Light
Shine inward, and the mind through all her powers
Irradiate, there plant eyes, all mist from these
Purge and disperse, that I may see and tell
Of things invisible to mortal sight.

(Milton, 1667, p. 64)

O and the mystic

This famous excerpt from Milton's *Paradise Lost*, about the loss of his sight, provides an idea of the intuition, the inner sight beyond the senses that Bion called O. His early idea of "binocular vision" reflected this function of our bicameral minds that was a sort of precursor to O, before Bion had actually conceived of that mystical idea. There are several such precursors to O in Bion's earlier theories of which he could not yet clearly conceive (cf. Reiner, 2022). These ideas, to use Bion's (1970, 1977) term, were still, for him, "thoughts without a thinker." Milton's words are a sort of incantation summoning up or exhorting the "celestial light" to "shine inward," very much as we might have to do as analysts if we are to see our way more clearly to that inner light. Artists in all of the Arts have their version of this in the idea of the "Muse," that mysterious source of inspiration, often felt to derive from something outside oneself, something or someone divine and beyond one's control. On the other hand, perhaps it is a way to give form to the infinite celestial or divine light that is part of our inherent mental potential. And so we hear of writers, painters and musicians' various versions of

DOI: 10.4324/9781003470953-4

"courting the Muse," attempts at coaxing one's creative spirit to emerge, as Milton did, but in ways ranging from contemplation, meditation and rituals, to caffeine, alcohol or drugs. Conversely, some religious sects "indulge" in abstention, abstaining from eating, or sexual activity, in order to break down the barriers to that realm of the spirit, a world beyond the body. Others use the body to do so, like the Whirling Dervishes, Sufi mystics who would dance and spin their way to ecstasy to the beat of rhythmic drums. One hopes that it is not necessary actually to go blind, as Milton did, to remove the distractions that obstruct inner sight. Freud (1916), however, also articulated the idea that to facilitate "seeing" into the Unconscious, he had to, "blind myself artificially in order to focus all the light on one dark spot" (p. 312). In a letter to Lou Andreas Salomé, he wrote:

[The analyst] must cast a beam of intense darkness so that something which has hitherto been obscured by the glare of illumination can glitter all the more in darkness.

(Freud, 1916, p. 312)

Although one does not literally have to be blind, one does have to find a way to block out the distractions illuminated in daylight, to cultivate the artificial blindness that allows one to see into inner life and into dreams, into the metaphysical realm of the mind.

Bion (1967b, 1970) suggests that one can gain access to O by suspending memory, desire and logical understanding, which is essentially another way of courting the Muse, trying to open one's mind to that higher self. In analytic terms, it provides access to a dreaming mind or self, while still maintaining contact with the waking mind or self. While getting drunk or taking drugs may imitate a dream state, it may also cause one to lose, or dull, one's other capacities for logical thinking that the analyst needs as well. As Rumi (1993) so aptly put it, "The man of God is drunken while sober" (p. 60). I think it may be useful to characterize O as a kind of Muse, by underlining the need to call upon a state of mind that is normally outside our control, but which facilitates psychoanalytic work by removing obstacles to deeper intuition. Only once we know that we *need* it to do our work, can we set out to find a way to make it happen. Whether it is called the Muse or Celestial Light or O, the psychoanalyst, like the poet or artist, needs to find a way to shift one's vision inward. It will inevitably include that sense of awe Bion described in the Introduction of his would-be book of poems. That feeling of awe is born of a broader, deeper intuitive realm of truth that is both admired and feared, often in equal measure. We may therefore retract from contact with it, and so must continually work toward overcoming this reticence to face these deeper truths. In analysis, however, O is not some kind of punishing external God, but a part of us that fears an often unfamiliar and unused aspect of our own minds.

As described above in the Introduction (p. 5), Bion was concerned that we were losing touch with the experience of awe, because of its uniquely challenging nature, but it seems especially true now in an increasingly technological world which offers countless distractions from the challenges of illuminating our inner lives. The profound, spiritual sense of awe that was always present in Bion's work was only later more clearly delineated in his concept of O. Two of the ways in which it was already present in his earlier theories was in his idea of maternal "reverie" as a requisite factor in the infant's development of the dream-like foundation of thinking he called "alpha function" (Bion, 1962, 1963). Without the ephemeral and amorphous capacity for reverie, that enables the mother to "dream" her child's emotional reality, the development of feeling, thinking and dreaming are obstructed. Only later with his concept of O, did Bion find a way to talk directly about it, but the precursors to these mystical concerns were clearly present before then (cf. Reiner, 2022).

> The analyst must focus his attention on O, the unknown and unknowable. The success of psycho-analysis depends on the maintenance of a psycho-analytic point of view; the point of view is the psycho-analytic vertex; the psycho-analytic vertex is O.
>
> (Bion, 1970, p. 27)

By putting forth the idea of O – of absolute truth or ultimate reality – as the central psychoanalytic perspective, this infinite unknown O was also given a place of central importance in Bion's theoretical work. Despite this, or maybe because of it, O became a lightning rod of controversy in psychoanalysis, in part because it represented an esoteric, unknown and unknowable reality, an infinite unconscious mind that is not only out of reach of our logical understanding, but also threatens our desire for certainty. Some of the controversy about this vast, transcendent unknown therefore seems to be *because* of the fact that it engenders such deep feelings of awe, thereby exposing us to the vast realm of our own ignorance. The aversion to this metaphysical perspective seems to endure, even though the vast unknowable Unconscious was central to psychoanalysis from its inception. Although there are ways in which O differs significantly from Freud's idea of the Unconscious, it also bears much in common with Freud's notion of an unknown and timeless metaphysical world. Bion's notion of O is not a dismissal of Freud's theory but rather an attempt to continue the necessary exploration that might help us to extend our theoretical and clinical knowledge of this vast unconscious realm embodied within us.

Bion's later teachings often stressed this need to continue learning, which then automatically puts us face to face with our ignorance.

> … [A]fter many years of effort, I have at last achieved the capacity to be awed by the depths of my ignorance… Such depths of ignorance are difficult to dare to contemplate. Therefore, I am bound to feel a wish to believe how god-like I am, how intelligent, as a change from being appalled at my ignorance.
>
> (Bion, 1974, p. 54)

Such unflinching awareness of one's ignorance is a by-product of real curiosity, and an experience of awe. Bion's association of O with a mystical state of mind is the aspect of O that has caused the greatest confusion and misapprehension. Over ten years ago, I was advised by a respected European psychoanalyst, greatly interested in Bion's work, not to mention this connection between O and the mystic. The main reason I never heeded this advice is that I do not see how the two can be separated, since this was the essence of the point Bion was making.

Religion, art, poetry, science

In this chapter, we will also see how this view of O is represented in poetry, art and science, as well as religion. First, however, since O is closely related to mystical religious ideas, and then often confused with traditional religion, I will first explore the misconceptions about what Bion *means* by "the mystic," and the ways in which he distinguishes it from organized religion. Given the relationship between O and the mystic, it is not surprising to find that Jesus, a Judeo-Christian mystic, described many of the same misconceptions about his ideas.

> Do not imagine that I have come to abolish the Law or the Prophets. I have come not to abolish but to fulfill them.
>
> (Gospel of Matthew 5:17)

Jesus goes on to say that his job is to teach the laws of the prophets anew, implying here, and elsewhere, that these ideas *need* to be taught, either because there is more to learn, or that they may not yet really have been learned in the first place. Similarly, as mentioned above, Bion's O is not a denial of Freud's idea of the Unconscious, but rather seeks to re-frame and extend Freud's discoveries, to further realize his ideas.

It is interesting that these "reminders" of things that were previously known, and sometimes for a very long time, can still be experienced as revolutionary, and still pose a threat to the status quo. It is true throughout history, and is certainly so with Bion's concept of O, which in some ways seeks to fulfill and update Freud's understanding of the Unconscious, as we may need better ways to understand and work with these known theories. In the process, such changes do alter that which was already known. Bion often pointed to the dangers of purely logical, theoretical understanding, for it is easy to learn theories intellectually, and to believe that theoretical knowledge means that one has really grasped its meaning and how to work with it. This is far from true, and it is that theoretical "knowledge" that Bion suggested the analyst had to put out of his mind, through the temporary suspension of one's memory, desire and understanding.

The gnostic gospels

The similarities and differences between traditional religious thought and the mystical notion of O, underlies much of the confusion about Bion's idea. But the mystic's ideas have often been subject to mis-perceptions, as they are often new ideas, challenging to the existing order. The Christian Gospels were written between 66 and 110 A.D., not too long after the death of Christ, but they told a very different story than the Gnostic Gospels, written slightly later, between 120 and 130 A.D. The former told the story of Christ as the literal son of God, and so a God himself. The Gnostics, on the other hand, were a mystical sect who took their name from the Latin, "gnosticus" and Greek "gnostos," relating to knowledge and knowing, and so they saw Jesus, not as a God but as a teacher of divine knowledge that each person had to learn for him- or herself (Pagels, 1979). From their perspective, the Christian view was a sort of concretization or reification of these ideas, a personification of the ideas in the man himself.

> The gnostic understands Christ's message not as offering a set of answers, but as encouragement to engage in a process of searching.
>
> (Pagels, 1989, p. 112)

The reified version of God in the Christian Gospels represents a reliance on an external omnipotent God, while the gnostic aim is to develop one's own capacity to learn these difficult truths. The Christian orthodoxy viewed the Gnostics as heretics, calling them "atheists" (Pagels, 1979, p. 83), while the Gnostics described those influenced by Orthodox Christians as "prisoners, for they are without perception" (Pagels, 1979, p. 112). This is very much the distinction Bion makes between repeating known theories rather than discovering these truths for oneself.

Freud's atheism shaped his ideas about religion in psychoanalytic thought, which may have contributed to some of the negative reactions to Bion's introduction of the mystical O into psychoanalysis.

Freud (1927) saw religion as a neurosis, or an illusion, reflecting the child's idealization of the parent. While Freud's view of religion was true as far as it went, it omits the idea of another aspect of mental functioning that goes beyond those primitive illusions of an external God. Bion's concept of O included another aspect of the mind capable of access to the wider spectrum of spiritual or divine knowledge.

Bion often pointed out that the job of the mystic is to put forth new ideas, even if they are actually old ideas that are "known" but may never have been emotionally understood or digested.

> It would be surprising if any true mystic were not regarded by the group as a mystical nihilist... It would be equally surprising if he were not in fact nihilistic to some group if for no other reason than that the nature of his contributions is certain to be destructive of the laws, conventions, culture, and therefore coherence of a group within the group, if not the whole group.
>
> (Bion, 1970, p. 64)

Bion's later theories, like O, were often a disturbance to his group of psychoanalysts, and in many cases have yet to be embraced as a theoretical or clinical tool. Bion often quotes Freud, upon whose work he bases much of his own, while also building on those theories to further our understanding. Bion says clearly:

Thinking, developed through psycho-analysis, has led to discoveries that were not made by Freud, but that reveal real configurations resembling those in discoveries he did make.

(Bion, 1970, p. 92)

Both scenarios require changes in the status quo. We may need to correct the misuses of an old theor that have become calcified in our minds over time, in, or we may need to go *beyond* the old idea because we have learned something new, or are still in need of learning something old that we mistakenly thought we already knew. In any of these instances, fear is generated that may lead to resistance, or even destruction of the new truth, or of the newly understood old truth, that is itself perceived as destructive to the ingrained beliefs that one wears as comfortably as an old pair of shoes.

The mystic and the genius

Is the implication in all this that Bion was a mystic? Kind of, but only if we use Bion's own definition of it. One way that Bion (1970) distinguished between the idea of mystical truth and the dogma of traditional religious practices, was by defining the term "mystic" as synonymous with, "genius" and "exceptional individual" (p. 64). He thereby broadens this intuitive mystical state to include a secular realm of any kind of creative genius, whether in the arts, sciences or in psychoanalysis, removing it from the strictly religious meaning. From this perspective of a mystic as someone with the clarity and vision of a genius, it is easier to see that we may need to include Bion in that category, despite the fact that he often insisted that he was not a mystic. However, from his earlier years in the British Psychoanalytic Society, and then its President, he was certainly recognized by many of his colleagues as a genius. He continued to be seen like that throughout the world, although there were always those, as I saw in Los Angeles, who thought instead that he was mad. As we know, in all these various disciplines, it is not unusual for geniuses to be considered madmen, and their works denied.

In a way it is understandable. Why would we mere mortals be expected easily to learn these profound esoteric mysteries of life? It is why Christ lamented the fact that many people, including his own apostles, did not have "ears to hear" (or understand) the arcane mysteries about which he spoke (Matthew 11:15). Nonetheless, these are critically important ideas, which is why Bion tirelessly reminded analysts of the deeper meanings behind the theories we often believe we already know, having fooled ourselves into thinking that stale theoretical knowledge can be applied to a patient's dynamic, living psyche. The logical part of the mind lacks the "ears to hear," or the heart to feel, those deeper meanings. We are then prone to try to convince ourselves of how "god-like" we are, as Bion said above, which unfortunately negates the sense of awe generated by actual contact with O, the absolute truth or divine knowledge. In traditional religious practices, one can easily engage in the *rituals* that may once have evolved from the passion and chaos of deeper religious experiences, rituals which begin to substitute rather than facilitate the real feeling. They can then only *symbolize* an experience, but in what Segal (1981) called a symbolic equation, that does not represent but rather *substitutes* for the experience. This is the opposite of what Bion meant by O.

That kind of splitting off of deeper emotional experience allows the mystic to be seen as equivalent to God, as Jesus was purported to be by overzealous "publicists" for the Christian Church. For Bion, the mystic, far from the image of an omniscient and omnipotent God, may be an intuitive person painfully aware of his impressive ignorance. O was described variously by Bion (1970) as absolute truth, ultimate reality and the Godhead. The differentiation between God and the Godhead will be examined below through the writings of Meister Eckhart, who used the term "Godhead" to represent the quest for one's own internal godhood, rather than the reification of an external God.

Infancy and awe

The deep sense of awe described above is the natural domain, not only of the mystic, but of the infant, for whom everything is new, vast and vastly mysterious, and for whom everything is unknown and unknowable. Infants embody this state in what Freud (1930) referred to as the infant's "oceanic feeling" (p. 64). They have no choice but to be one with experiences for which they do not yet have any context or understanding, and more importantly, do not yet have a sense of self that might afford them any defenses or barriers against their experiences. The infant's boundless oceanic mind is the seat of that pure and awesome experience, which fills them with emotions as yet uncontained by thought and reason. As adults, it is challenging, and can be dangerous, to allow ourselves to drop down into that primal, egoless mind, and yet this is essentially what Bion suggested as the necessary state of mind for doing psychoanalytic work, by suspending memory, desire and understanding.

Although the analyst in contact with O retains contact with that primal infant mind, it is not equivalent to O. The infant's experience differs from what Bion described as the analyst's experience of O, in that the analyst must also simultaneously employ more evolved capacities to think, to contain and express emotional experiences. Bion (1965, 1970) described this as a transformation from O to K (Knowledge). It is for this reason that infants do not make good analysts, for while contact with O requires contact with that infant mind, it is more than *just* that primal perspective. We could say that *the infant's capacity for primal oneness with the object, or any other experience, is a necessary but not sufficient condition for analytic work*. Therefore, according to Bion, analytic work cannot be done without access to that primal infantile state, but it also requires of the analyst, the development of, and access to, the more sophisticated mental functions of an individuated mind. This simultaneous functioning of those two essentially opposing states of mind is reflected in Rumi's (1993) description of the mystic mentioned above "The man of God is drunken while sober" (p. 60). Metaphorically speaking, the infant in that primal oceanic mind (O) might be said to be "drunk," awash in a purely experiential, boundaryless dream-like mind, but like Rumi's "man of God," or the psychoanalyst, one must at the same time be "sober," with the capacity to withstand and think about the chaos of that disorganized state without drowning or being swept away. This state of mind is also suggested in Bion's idea of Ps:D, which he saw as the continuous fluctuations between the primitive (paranoid-schizoid) and more organized (depressive) functions of the mind. He also viewed this fluctuation from the disorganized primal state to the organized mind, as necessary in the creation of any interpretation.

> No analyst is entitled to believe that he has done the work required to give an interpretation unless he has passed through both phases.
>
> (Bion, 1970, p. 124)

This process is much like the gnostic idea that one cannot just memorize the ideas of the master, or of God, but must continue to engage in the work of one's own learning at every step.

Secular mysticism

Despite the tendency to equate O to traditional religion, Bion's mystical concept represents a kind of "secular mysticism," a mystical state of mind which includes a scientific perspective. Examples of secular mystics would certainly include Einstein, as well as Bion, both of whom would be considered atheists, *vis-á-vis* traditional religious beliefs, despite their strong sense of the mystical.

> The cosmic religious experience is the strongest and noblest mainspring of scientific research.
>
> (Einstein, 1952, p. 117)

For Einstein, as for Bion, the "cosmic religious experience" is not the belief in religious dogma, or reliance on faith in a reified, anthropomorphic God, *rather it is the natural experience of awe and wonder* when faced with the vast, inexplicable order of the universe. The reified God serves as a buffer between that mystical knowledge and one's own mind. Bion's repeated insistence that O was part of a scientific perspective, is in line with Einstein's religious views.

> I cannot conceive of a true scientist without that profound faith... Science without religion is lame, religion without science is blind.
>
> (Einstein, 1950, p. 26).

It is the two in tandem that facilitates this experience of faith. It reflects another marriage of seemingly opposing mental functions, a *relationship* between two different states, without which the mind cannot operate at its highest level.

It is the most important function of art and science to awaken [the cosmic religious] feeling and keep it alive in those who are receptive to it.

(Einstein, 1954, p. 48)

Einstein views this mystical sense as beyond the scope of traditional religion, and also alludes to the common aims of art and science in keeping it alive. I found Einstein's addendum to this statement interesting, about keeping this expansive sense of awe alive, "in those who are receptive to it." It brought to mind the some-times less than enthusiastic reactions to Bion's introduction of the cosmic, mystical perspective into psychoanalysis. Since I saw the value in it, and had seen how it worked both with my patients and in my own analysis, I felt a certain urgency to stress the importance of this concept in my own work and writings. However, I was not yet wise enough to keep in mind Einstein's understanding that not everyone is receptive to it. Bion has been lauded for the brilliance of his ideas throughout the psychoanalytic world, but some of these ideas cannot readily be grasped, or grasped at all, which understandably can frustrate, or frighten, people. Nonethe-less, it seems important to recognize that those with an avid interest in Bion's work, who are dismissive of his concept of O, may have overlooked the fact that their interest in Bion's work omits what he viewed as the central psychoanalytic perspective. Some go so far as to view this later idea of the mystical state of O as a *betrayal* of his earlier work, rather than as a continuation and *fulfillment* of it (Reiner, 2022).

Grotstein clearly addresses the confusion and controversy over Bion's associa-tion between O and the mind of the mystic.

Most critics of Bion's postulation of O fault him for what they believe is his religiosity. Nothing could be further from the truth.

(Grotstein, 2007, p. 231)

While it is true that Bion was not traditionally religious, describing O as "secular mysticism" has sometimes been mistaken to mean that it is not therefore mystical or religious. To the contrary, I think it is both mystical *and* religious, if we con-sider that institutionalized religions cannot necessarily be considered to be truly religious. Nietzsche (1887) put it this way, "The religious person is an exception in every religion" (p. 185). The mystics are often the exceptions, the outliers who dare to question the religious orders with which they are affiliated. As we will soon see, this was the case with Meister Eckhart.

Bion's (1970) idea of "faith" as a necessary part of the work of psychoanalysis is differentiated from religious faith in an external God. For Bion, faith, which he denotes as "F," represents a faith in the existence of Truth, even if we do not know the truth in that moment. That, of course, is when we need faith, when we do not know the answers, but are able to remain open enough to believe that there *is* a cogent answer, and that there is such thing as the kind of absolute truth of O. One might think that this is obvious, and that all analysts have faith in the existence of truth, but if this were so, Bion would not have had the need to postulate O. Nor would there be such backlash to this level of truth. It represents faith in intuition, a nonlogical means to that truth, upon which seekers after truth – like mystics, artists or scientists – may have to rely. About this intuitive state, Jung wrote:

> The Germans call this an Einfall, which means a thing which falls into your head from nowhere... like a revelation.
>
> (Jung, 1935, p. 15)

Although he describes it as a "revelation," connoting a religious experience, Jung goes on to call it, "...a very natural function, a perfectly normal thing" (Jung, 1935, p. 15). It is similar to Bion's (1978) idea of "wild thoughts," "thoughts without a thinker" that might similarly be said to "fall into your head," if you don't lose faith. And that while mysterious, it is perfectly natural.

Bion (1970) made the point that people's tendency to link faith with the supernatural was a "distortion," and he attributed this view to "a lack of experience of the 'natural' to which it relates" (p. 48). For Bion faith was "an essential component of scientific procedure" (1970, p. 43). For Einstein as well, it is associated with the sense of awe – a non-denominational, non-institutional religious feeling when faced with the vast order of all that we cannot fathom. While it inevitably arouses feelings of being small, insignificant and ignorant, it is the state of mind that Bion suggests cultivating if we are to gain access to O – the unknown and unknowable absolute truth. We may be small and ignorant, but this does not mean that truth does not exist, and it is our faith in the existence of truth, our patience and ability to tolerate the frustration of not knowing it, that may eventually enable us to intuit its existence. This ability to embrace our ignorance, and believe in the existence of truth is the foundation of awe, the kind of mystical sense that is the source of artistic, scientific, religious and psychoanalytic truth. Bion wrote:

> Thanks to Faraday and other scientists ordinary people can illuminate a room by the touch of a switch; thanks to Freud and his co-workers, ordinary people hope by psycho-analysis to be able to illuminate the mind. The fact that the world's work has to be done by ordinary people makes this work of scientification (or vulgarization, or simplification, or communication...) imperative. There are not enough mystics and those that there are must not be wasted.
>
> (Bion, 1970, pp. 79–80)

In an earlier writing, although published later, Bion (1989) described this idea slightly differently, referring to Faraday as a genius who could "demonstrate the reality of electricity so that people of less messianic capacity can switch on an electric light" (p. 32). About religious feeling, he continues, "It takes a mystic to demonstrate the existence of God so that people who lack that endowment can understand enough to know when and how to switch on the appropriate ritual and employ the correct magic" (p. 32).

Unfortunately, most of us have to count ourselves among the "ordinary people," which no one likes to do, and which may be the biggest source of unpopularity for O. However, from whatever point we start, we can all strive to do better, and if we can sufficiently tame our arrogance or envy, perhaps we can even develop intermittent access to this kind of intuitive knowledge. One thing seems clear, it cannot be done by magic, or the magic of associating ourselves with religious or scientific geniuses. Religious rituals are designed to coax the mind into that spiritual sense of awe, and through the grandeur of art, architecture, heavenly music and fragrant incense may at times even succeed in doing so. Alternatively, they may be coerced by intimidation, guilt and the fear of infernal punishment – into an experience of the dark side of awe. However, rituals often become rigid, proformative versions of these feelings, that are a kind of facsimile of awe, a parody of true religious feeling that lacks its more profound emotional foundation. The fate of many revolutionary ideas is to become a widely accepted version of the real thing, the acceptable dogma of a new Establishment that lacks the vitality and potency of the original idea. As Bion (1989) wrote, "So-called Scientific Laws are vulgarizations of that which the scientific mystic can achieve directly" (p. 32).

Bion raised the question as to whether the vulgarized or popularized versions of the messianic idea can actually succeed in psychoanalysis. He believed that merely learning the old theories of our revered predecessors will not help us in our work with an actual patient. One must be able to feel and think for oneself. Recognizing the importance of geniuses and mystics who have these special gifts also presents the larger group with difficult feelings of envy, which instead impedes our efforts to try to learn from these mentors how we might open ourselves up to a broader view. Not everyone has the same intuitive gifts, which makes the concept of O a decidedly non-democratic view. While one might think we would be grateful for someone who can help us to see further, instead it often engenders feelings of fear, inadequacy and hatred in the face of an unknown one cannot grasp. While many analysts at Bion's Los Angeles lectures in the 1970s proclaimed that he was psychotic, thereby eradicating whatever might be deemed enviable, it seems wise to remember Bion's (1970) advice, "There are not enough mystics and those that there are must not be wasted" (p. 80).

The unseen in Rumi and Bion

We will look now at the works of Jelaluddin Rumi, the 13th century Sufi mystic, and Hafiz, another beloved Persian poet and mystic from the 14th century, which shed light on Bion's essential idea of O. Their poems, along with excerpts from *The Bhagavadgita,* will provide another experiential perspective on O.

Out beyond duality,
we have a home, and it is Glory.
That pure substance is
different from this dusty world.

What kind of place is this?...
This is the time of union,
the time of eternal beauty...
it is the light of God...
Beyond this world is a world
that has no boundaries....
This light is at once joined
with all things, and yet apart from all.
                        (Rumi, 1981, pp. 36–38)

While this "world without boundaries" is familiar to analysts as the timeless unconscious, Rumi's description of the transcendent mind sounds like a much more ecstatic state than we usually associate with psychoanalysis. Indeed, it is closer to Bion's transcendent mind of O. However, while mystical poets like Rumi use the language of religion, their message is beyond the ideas of traditional religions. In order to cultivate a mind free from the judgments, expectations and previously learned knowledge of any dogma, one must focus on one's own access to new moments of enlightenment. That place "beyond duality" is a state of oneness and integration which can only come with one's awareness of states of dis-integration and separation from one's higher self. We can experience wholeness only if we know we are divided, and this pure state often affords us just a fleeting access to that unity. Still, despite our finite ego in a world of limits and boundaries, we do have the potential for access to the infinite, "out beyond duality... at once joined with all things, and yet apart from all." The deep intuition of Bion's waking-dream state of O reflects the unity of a mind, "beyond duality," capable of access to intuitive dream states beyond the logical mind. Blake here reflects on similar ideas.

> If the doors of perception were cleansed everything would appear to man as it is, infinite.
> For Man has closed himself up, till he sees all things thro' narrow chinks of his cavern.
>
>   (Blake, 1790–93, p. 56)

Although Rumi was a Sufi – a Persian Islamic mystic – he also wrote about Jesus and other Christian prophets as purveyors of the same knowledge. For Rumi, God is variously described as Love, the Beloved, the Friend, the Teacher, all secular words referring to human emotional connections. Hafiz made similarly secular references to God as Master, Friend, Lover, Companion and Guide, and referred to himself as a servant of God's message. Each of these visionaries is speaking of a human realm of the divine, rather than an omnipotent, anthropomorphic *external* God, and about the awesome universal truths with which we can engage if we can transcend our finite minds. Á propos of this, Grotstein

(2007) referred to O as the "transcendent position," beyond Klein's schizoid and depressive positions (p. 97, fn. 2).

The religious concerns of Rumi and Hafiz also reflect the domains of Art and science, all of which aim to provide means to access the transcendent experiences of truth and beauty. For Bion it is achieved through the mental discipline of suspending memory, desire and understanding, but Rumi's paradoxical statement below also addresses this challenging process.

> You will never find anything until you seek—except this beloved, whom you will not seek until you find.
>
> (Rumi, 1994, p. 198)

He implies a sort of spontaneous, unexpected experience, a visitation from a source that cannot actively be sought. Like the idea of the Muse, it is out of one's control. If one forfeits control, one might then learn to be prepared for this experience. Neither the Muse, O, the "Beloved," or God, is attained through conscious or active means, but rather by letting go of one's ego, relinquishing one's already known self, an effort which is the opposite of seeking *for* something. It is very much what Keats (1817) described as "Negative Capability" for which he felt that certain great writers, like Shakespeare, have an affinity. He described it as, "The capacity to be in uncertainties, mysteries, doubts, without any irritable reaching after fact or reason" (p. 329). Rather than seeking to *do* or *know* something, one must learn to tolerate, and embrace, not knowing. The analyst, likewise, must seek *not* to do, want, remember, or know anything, but merely to be an open vessel. It is essentially the opposite to how we are taught to learn, retain and apply knowledge. This seemingly emptied mind, however, is not exactly empty. It is not even a space exactly, but rather a sort of potential space created in the process of becoming a conduit for whatever previously unknown truth exists in the moment. By suspending one's search for already known facts, one cultivates a receptive mental space for whatever might emerge, much as a dream image emerges from within us.

No wonder people were angry at Bion, for one is essentially being asked to give up one's beloved ego, the active do-er and know-er by which most people define themselves, for this seemingly passive dreamer. Each person has to find his or her way to experience this state of mind beyond logic, and first to find a way of knowing what it feels like. It may seem daunting, or impossible, and yet we do have the familiar prototype of our dreams, which occur in the same way, without our conscious efforts.

Signs of the Unseen: Discourses of Jalaluddin Rumi, is a collection of Rumi's poems, prose discourses and conversations from 1317 A.D. (Thackston, 1994, p. xiv). "Signs of the unseen" is the phrase written on the cover of Rumi's notebook, which is a translation of the Arabic title which literally means, "in it what is in it." In part, this is a reference to the casual nature of Rumi's miscellaneous writings, but it also reflects the paradoxical nature of that experience of knowledge that cannot be known or controlled by our conscious minds, the signs for which are available to the intuitive mind.

The title reminded me of Moses who, upon asking God His name on Mount Sinai, is told, "I Am Who I Am" (Exodus 3: 14). This tautological proclamation reflects the undefinable essence of existence, the unknowable noumenon of Kant's idea of the "thing-in-itself." Like the essentially indescribable O that cannot be represented or known, it just is what it is. The Negative Capability at the heart of these ideas is reflected in these words by Hafiz.

> *I am a hole in a flute that the Christ's breath*
> *moves through—listen to this music.*

> (Hafiz, 2011, p. 3)

It is not one's ego that facilitates a sense of the divine or mystical truth, but the capacity to relinquish control of one's self in order to be one with whatever is there to be known.

Wisdom or oblivion

O is a tricky state to contemplate or achieve, for if one is truly asleep, one runs the risk of *descending* into oblivion instead of *ascending* to a divine awareness, a common confusion which we see in our patients, and ourselves. Rumi alludes to something of this confusion as well.

> *If you eat sweets and roast meat or drink pure wine,*
> *you will dream of drinking water.*
> *But you will awake from your dream thirsty.*
> *Dream water quenches no thirst.*
> (Rumi 1994, p. 194)

Rumi explains that to desire worldly things is like being given something in a dream. And yet, if one can manage the discipline suggested by Bion, of being a *waking* dreamer, one gains access to a world of meaning beyond sense-based experiences. Rumi writes:

> *I have discovered...*
> *that he who is my sustenance will come to me.*
> *I run to him, and my quest for him is agony for me.*
> *Were I to sit still,*
> *he would come to me without my distress*
> (Rumi, 1994, p. 192)

Countless other seers, poets, philosophers and artists have said versions of the same thing, like Milton (1650) who wrote in his Sonnet on his blindness:

...God doth not need
Either man's work or his own gifts. Who best
Bear his mild yoke, they serve him best...
They also serve who only stand and wait.
(Milton, 1650, p. 107)

It is along the lines of Negative Capability, as are Rumi's words above, which also reflect Bion's idea that one cannot know O, but one can *become* it, again by relinquishing one's ego, in the process of which one might become the truth of that moment. And again, similarly, Christ tells his disciples:

Whoever wants to be a follower of mine, let him renounce himself and....follow me... Anyone who loses his life for my sake will find it.
(Matthew 16: 24–26)

From a secular religious perspective, Christ here is a symbol of the mystical or divine Truth, and he appeals to them to follow this higher Truth. Giving up everything is to embrace the empty or egoless mind of O, the Negative Capability that enables the mind to receive these deeper Truths that we otherwise know little about. Along these same lines Rumi writes:

I saw the Friend clearly, and I stopped reading
books and memorizing poems.
I quit going to church, and I quit fasting
to be a better person.
I quit worrying about when I should be praying.
I saw how I was undisciplined and toxic.
I saw how lovely and strong.
(Rumi, 1984, p. 60)

It is a question of how to be what one is, and not what one wants to be. Established religious rituals and dogma are symbolic of the divine, but can become substitutes that obstruct the ability to find one's own truth. Contact with the God that Rumi calls the Friend, depends on letting go of externally imposed rules, just as Bion suggests forgetting the theories of psychoanalysis that can cloud one's vision of the moment one inhabits. Rumi's advice, to quit the Church, stop reading books and stop performing prescribed rituals, are in line with Bion's suggestions that analysts stop praying at the Church of Psychoanalysis so that they can see and feel for themselves. It takes a very different kind of discipline to find one's own path to that state of mind, than the discipline of performing established versions of rituals blessed by these institutions. These are revolutionary ideas of post-religious religions, which suggest that what is important is not merely to learn what the pundits teach, but the need to find one's way to whatever can impart an experience of these religious feelings of awe.

Fernando Pessoa was a mystical Portuguese poet of the 20th century, whose work will be more fully examined in Chapter 4, but I include this one paragraph here, as it illustrates the paradoxical sense, as Christ described, of losing oneself, or losing one's life, to gain this other kind of inner life.

> Like all great enthusiasts, I love the delight of losing myself, in which I suffer the pleasure of giving myself over totally. And so, many times, I write without wanting to think, in an external daydreaming, allowing the words to play around me... They are sentences without meaning, softly flowing, in a fluidity of felt water, a forgetting of oneself on the shore.
>
> (Pessoa, 1931, p. 9)

This idea of "losing" oneself is an essential part of the mystic's, or the artist's, waking-dream state. For the psychoanalyst it reflects the difficult discipline of suspending one's ego functions of memory, desire and understanding, that Bion described as the path to O. One thereby leaves *knowing* behind and enters a world of *being*. In that world, even words, according to Pessoa, no longer have the meanings assigned to them in our normal use of language, words that evolved to deal with the phenomenological world of the senses. In poems, words adopt new meaning in their playful, symbolic and associative interactions with other words, much like the words and images in dreams create a new use of language that evokes a numinous world of unconscious meanings.

Pessoa's paradoxical description of "suffering the pleasure" of this state, is very much like Bion's (1970) idea that both pain *and* pleasure need to be "suffered" in order truly to be felt (p. 19). I think this reflects the idea of an inherent existential suffering in a state of being, for a true ontological experience of one's feelings is always based on the capacity for separateness, an acceptance of one's existential aloneness, even from those we love.

I can give an example of that watery fluidity of words and sentences to which Pessoa alluded in a poem that emerged to express a similar idea. It is familiar to me in my experience when writing or painting. In fact, there have been times when someone asks if I have written any poems lately, and I found myself saying, "Not really." However, I would later recall that I had in fact written a poem just that day, sometimes even a long poem, about which I had completely forgotten. Because it had been written in that dream state where the sentences, as Pessoa said, were "without meaning, softly flowing, in a fluidity of water..." I had no idea at that time, what the poem was about, or what those words were actually saying, and apparently I did not even recollect having written it at all. It is not unlike the very common experience of forgetting one had a dream, which then sometime in the day, floats up into consciousness. In such cases, we were asleep when we "created" the dream and our waking selves have no awareness of it. With a poem I was only half-asleep, but enough for the words to have this very different quality. Only when going back to read it while fully awake, did I learn that I had indeed said something with meaning, or that something had somehow been said *for* me, as if my role there was as some sort of passive amanuensis for something that was being dictated to me. Here is one such poem that I not only wrote while not fully aware of having written it, but it is also *about* that dream-like experience.

Boddhisatva Gets the News

The dark is invisible
if you don't know the Lights are off.
It is hard to see the Light
if you cannot see the dark.
You are sleeping, blind
until the no-Light finally turns on
and shocks your eyes,
while you stare in dumb surprise.
You look past the veil, beyond the scrim
at a world you thought was a foreign film
in which you, at best,
were a minor character on someone else's quest.
It makes you think,
but you don't know how to think,
though it is your job,
so you just continue staring
in the direction of Something
that might eventually come,
Someone who might speak to you
loud and slow
about Something you both
Somehow need to know.
Meanwhile, I'll keep talking to myself,
for now that the Light is on,
I can listen.

(Reiner, 2023, unpublished)

The experience of losing oneself in a search for Truth is the same, whether writing a poem, or following a teacher like Christ or Mohammed, or trying to apprehend the ultimate reality in a session with a patient. In each case, one has to let go of one's knowing self to allow the mind to open to something new.

Hafiz

Some of the 14th century poems of Hafiz sound like interpretations to buried souls who do not know they are buried. His efforts to disinter these souls and give them new life, sound like the psychoanalyst's effort to find the abandoned infant-self imprisoned in an invisible mental prison or crypt, a dead soul whom the analyst, or the poet, may intuitively "hear" screaming in pain. Although these poems are not connected to any psychoanalytic theory, they do closely reflect what we can sense as deep psychical states. Again, it also sounds like Winnicott's (1960) idea of the False Self, a mask beneath which is buried an unknown True Self, whose suffering has become umbed and insensible, a self secretly unknown even to oneself. In the following poem, Hafiz, like the psychoanalyst, tries to speak to and engage that troubled mind, self or soul (terms Bion uses interchangeably) that unconsciously aches for life, connection and love.

Cast All Your Votes for Dancing

I know the voice of depression
Still calls to you.
I know those habits that can ruin your life
Still send their invitations.
Keep squeezing drops of the Sun
From your prayers and work and music...
Learn to recognize the counterfeit coins
That may buy you just a moment of pleasure
But then drag you for days
Like a broken man
Behind a farting camel.

(Hafiz, 2006, pp. 8–9)

It is not unusual to see people, including analytic patients, who spend "counterfeit coins" that buy what are perceived to be moments of pleasure, whether through drugs, alcohol, food or sex. In fact, they are just distractions from the unknown, but nagging unconscious pain of that deadened state. This includes addictions, not only to substances, but addictions to earlier traumas and early states of mind that spawned early though untenable beliefs, unconsciously created to "protect" the infant from the pain of neglect, abuse or feelings that could not be felt or digested. The frustrated desires for a loving connection are replaced by the addictive substance or ideas, false desires that are essentially unquenchable, if one has been robbed of the awareness of one's actual needs. These "habits that can ruin your life still send their invitations," as Hafiz put it, they are still trying to seduce the individual with false promises to heal the pain, but whatever momentary peace they provide are in fact starving the mind and the self of reality, and of truth. As we see all the time in psychoanalytic work, these old "invitations" can feel impossible to refuse, as they are bound up in the infant's ancient contracts with a primitive superego whose promises of freedom from pain actually deliver only the death of the real self (Reiner, 2009). This is a very different way of "losing oneself," that is opposite to Pessoa's experience of losing himself in the creative process that may help in awareness and expression of the pain. It is also opposite to Christ's promise that his followers will lose their lives, which is really to gain their lives if they follow the path of truth, and the truth that Bion called

O. All of these represent a temporary denial of the sense-based ego, in the service of facilitating access to a deeper self and mind. The infant's unconscious covenant with an omnipotent superego/God, offers the empty promise of deliverance from pain as a defense against reality, before the infant has developed the capacity to apprehend reality. It is not, like the analyst's O, the *temporary suspension of ego functions*, but rather a measure taken before there is a mind capable of ego functions, which can suspend the development of those ego functions forever.

For the most part, we cannot speak for the methods of religious mystics or artistic or scientific geniuses, for there is probably a big spectrum of capacities for consciousness in such people, despite their intuitive or artistic gifts. But Bion's idea of O clearly delineates the need for both these mental capacities, an inclusive relationship between that dream-like intuitive suspension of logic, and the functions of a more reason-driven ego, able to work together. The analyst must use both that intuitive mind of O, as well as the ego functions that lead to the kind of knowledge we can communicate to the patient, that Bion represented as "K" (cf. Reiner, 2022, pp. 71–73).

> The psycho-analyst is concerned with O, which is incommunicable save through K activity. O may appear to be attainable by K through phenomena, but in fact that is not so, Ke depends on the evolution O Y K.
>
> (Bion, 1970, p. 30)

Both states of mind are necessary in making an analytic interpretation, and so "losing oneself" does not mean the complete absence of that rational aspect of mental functioning. The infant has not yet developed this capacity for knowledge, and so once he or she loses touch with the emotional self, it may be lost forever, unless they are helped to retrieve it. It is lost in those promises to which people are then programmed to cling for their whole lives. Since the mind or self has not yet developed, in effect they have lost the *potential* for a mind. They are addicted to what Hafiz called "counterfeit coins," which seem valuable but which in fact lead only to being forever dragged behind "a farting camel."

Clinical vignette – Mrs. A

One patient, Mrs. A, whose mother was infantile and depressed, fought all her life to fix her mother, in the hope that her mother would then become the loving mother she so needed. Mrs. A never gave up the hope, garnered from that early unconscious covenant, that if she saved her mother, she too would be saved. She recreated this scenario in her marriage to a husband she loved, but who was too troubled himself to be responsible to her needs. She recreated that endless journey from despair to hope to disappointment, anger and despair, and then it would start all over again. After seven years of analysis, she was exhausted, and finally could stop the cycle long enough to realize that the real feeling was sadness and helplessness that she had put her faith in the wrong person, first in her mother, and then a husband equally unable to be what she needed. Able to see that she had chosen this husband, in part because she had to bring this whole dynamic to light, she took one step away from that vicious cycle that had been repeating for five decades.

This could not be more common. It is important to distinguish between O – the contact with a higher intuitive mind – and that omnipotent God/parent in whom Mrs. A put her faith as an infant. The latter amounts to a confusion between the life and death of the self or mind, with no way to determine if one's loyalty to that omnipotent God is a "cure" or a denial of reality and Truth. It is a difficult distinction to make in that invisible realm of the infant mind where truth and lies have never been differentiated. Perhaps nobody put it more plainly and succinctly than Emily Dickinson.

> *Much Madness is divinest Sense –*
> *To a discerning Eye –*
> *Much Sense – the starkest Madness –*
> *'Tis the Majority*
> *In this, as All, prevail –*
> *Assent – and you are sane –*
> *Demur – you're straightaway dangerous –*
> *And handled with a Chain –*
> (Dickinson, 1890, p. 38)

Meister Eckhart – god vs. the godhead

Bion's inclusion of the more secular terms of "genius" and "exceptional person" in the same realm as the mystic, is similar to the distinction he makes in defining O as the "Godhead" rather than the God of religious institutions. He makes this distinction with reference to the ideas of Meister Eckhard, a medieval German mystic and complex, radical thinker. Some of his ideas, including his use of the term, "Godhead" to differentiate it from the God of the Church, veered from Church orthodoxy in ways that in 1326 got him condemned by religious leaders who feared his teachings would turn people away from the Church (Eckhart, 1994, p. xiv). "Godhead," from the German word, "*gottheit*," meaning "godhood" or "godliness," implies an individual quest, for as Eckhart (1941) said, "God is known through God in the soul" (p. 160). This inner "God" is a part of one's own divine nature, not an external, omnipotent judge of one's spiritual value. He was talking about, "something uncreated, divine in the soul" (p. xxvii), and it was man's work to 'find' or experience this God within oneself. This decidedly more human approach was also evident in his idea, "*Esse est Deus*" [Being is God] (Eckhart, 1941, Note 10, p. 322), but it was an approach that was viewed as heresy. In keeping with the tendency of religions to find true mystics to be heretics, Eckhart was indeed prosecuted by the Archbishop of Cologne and found, after his death, to be a heretic (Eckhart, 1941, p. xxiv).

The following is part of a sermon given by Eckhart. He is discussing here Christ's sermon on the mount, "Blessed are the poor in spirit, theirs is the kingdom of heaven" (Matthew 5:3).

> [W]e say that a poor person is someone who desires nothing. Some people do not understand this point correctly… those who cling to their own egos in their penances and external devotions. God have mercy on them, for they know little of the divine truth! These people are called holy because of what they are seen to do, but inside they are asses, for they do not know the real meaning of divine truth… These people… mean well and that is why they deserve our praise. May God in his mercy grant them heaven! But I tell you by the divine truth that such people are not truly poor… I tell you that they are asses, who understand nothing of God's truth.
>
> (Eckhart, 1994, pp. 203–204)

While one can see why such mystics may be unpopular with the Institutions they are meant to represent, they are talking about aspects of human minds and souls that are not visible or otherwise obvious to the senses. Eckhart differentiates this "divine truth" from the teachings of the Church, the difference between true wisdom and the *appearance* of wisdom. As we will examine in Chapter 5, it is the same idea that led Nietzsche (1887) to his famous conclusion, "God is dead," which for him meant that the Christian Church had killed or destroyed the true understanding of God as a representation of that divine knowledge that is the heart of authentic morality, conscience and consciousness (pp. 181–182).

Eckhart (1994) relates the story of Saint Augustine who, when asked what eternal life might be, replied, "You ask me what eternal life is? You had better ask eternal life itself" (p. 165). That is O, aiming toward direct experience of the divine which, like absolute truth or Kant's "thing-in-itself," is ultimately impossible.

Clearly, these are not new ideas, but they are the essence of the concept of O. Eckhart's distinction is the same one Bion makes between *being* an analyst (or anything else) and being in an on-going process of *becoming* an analyst (or whatever one aspires to). It is an internal distinction, for the truly "poor in spirit" have eschewed the presumed "wealth" of the knowledge of the ego, in favor of that same sense of impoverishment inherent in the emptiness of daring not to know. Like Pessoa's (1931) idea of "a forgetting of oneself on the shore" (p. 9), or the idea that contact with O is achieved by emptying the mind of memory, desire and understanding, Eckhart talks of this self-imposed emptiness, and the need for detachment from the things of this world, if one is to find that sense of the divine in oneself.

The Bhagavadgita

If these seem like rarified, esoteric ideas that do not apply to everyday people, we have only to look at the great Hindu text of *The Bhagavadgita* (1979) to see the universality of these ideas in everyday life. The story of the *Bhagavadgita*, meaning "Song of the Lord," begins with Arjuna, a young warrior about to go into battle, but when he comes face to face with the enemy, he is shocked to find members of his own family within their ranks. Seeing his uncles, brothers, father, sons and beloved mentors and friends, Arjuna feels dizzy, frightened and overwhelmed, and sinks down in despair and confusion. Having lost all desire for victory, he cannot go on. He is helped by his charioteer, Krsna, who turns out to be the Lord, Krishna, who begins to enlighten the young warrior to a realm of divine knowledge that is invisible, imperishable and eternal.

Arjuna's ancient dilemma is one that psychoanalysts face in their patients every day, namely the plight of the inner child who struggles mightily with his own warring forces of love and hate toward his parents. It is at the heart of Melanie Klein's (1937) theories about the good and bad breast (or mother), and the good and bad aspect of the child, the fight between the unconscious pain and the guilt of seeing one's loved ones as objects of hatred. This battle probably plays out in as many ways as there are people, but it is essentially the same struggle for a separate self, a struggle for conscience that, according to Klein (1946) resolves in the achievement of the depressive position.

The divine knowledge set forth to Arjuna in *The Bhagavadgita* differs from the techniques used in analytic work, but is contained in Bion's addition to Klein's paranoid-schizoid and depressive positions is his development of O, which does include the states of mind about which Krishna tries to educate Arjuna. Grotstein wrote:

> ... Bion's concept of O both transcends and precedes and succeeds Klein's concept of the paranoid-schizoid and depressive positions.
>
> (Grotstein, 2007, p. 121)

However, while Klein spoke of good internal objects as a strength and important aspect of a sense of self, some analysts, like Fairbairn (1944) see even these so-called "good" internal objects as evidence of a schism in the self. Grotstein called O the "transcendent position," a path to wholeness and consciousness, achieved through Keats' (1917) idea of negative capability which is an eschewal of the ego in the process of becoming one with absolute truth. This is the state of mind about which Krishna schools Arjuna, a state of mind beyond the primal attachments to the parents, to a broader understanding of what it means to exist in a more evolved truth, in one's internal and external reality.

Every child's individuation is similar to Arjuna's search for one's higher self or mind, a complex fight for freedom from "internal objects" laid down in the self before one can think or assess the meaning and consequences of those attachments. This is the battle, and the source of the vertiginous confusion that ensues for Arjuna as he sets out to go beyond those early, primitive identifications to find his own unique mind and self.

Each child, to greater or lesser degrees depending on the level of infantile trauma they may have suffered, is forced to go against his own mother and his own father to achieve his own mind. While this struggle is dramatized by the two armies facing off before each other in *The Bhagavadgita*, the inner struggle is probably equally "bloody," at least symbolically, if one is to experience the birth of one's real emotional self or mind, which is also the birth of one's "godhood," a different self than suggested by the achievement of Klein's depressive position.

This is an excerpt from *The Bhagavadgita*, which has been used in India as a source of meditation and wisdom since the 2nd or 3rd century B.C. The Lord, Krishna, here describes to Arjuna, the means of access to a spiritual realm, which is the terrain of "a man of judgment."

> *A man is of firm judgement*
> *when he has abandoned all inner desires...*
> *When unpleasant things do not perturb him*
> *nor pleasures beguile him...*
> *That man has a firm judgement*
> *who feels no desire toward anything.*
> *Whatever good or bad he incurs,*
> *he never delights in it nor hates it.*
> (*The Bhagavadgita*, 1979, p. 33)

Krishna then describes the man of judgment as one who "withdraws his senses from the sensual world," all of which are very much in line with Bion's characterization of O as a state of mind beyond sense-based reality, and beyond memory and desire. By suspending thoughts of the past (memory) and of the future (desire), one removes the impediments to being in the present.

Bion (1965) wrote, "[O] is not good or evil; it cannot be known, loved or hated" (p. 139).

The idea of O that is neither good nor evil reflects the idea that the truth is simply the truth, and that O – ultimate reality or absolute truth – simply *Is*. It is not to be judged and, as Rumi said (above, p. 10), it is "out beyond duality." It represents an ontological state of being, an area of study that Heidegger (1927) was at great pains to describe, although he viewed the issue of Being as "*the* fundamental question" (p. 3).

Bion describes the belief of many psychologists and philosophers, including Plato, Kant, Freud and Klein, that a veil of illusion separates us from reality, but he goes on to suggest that "...mystics must be exempted from this belief of inaccessibility to absolute reality" (Bion, 1965, p. 147). It is not only that *reality* is impossible to apprehend, but our mental apparatus is also limited, especially if we continue to use the wrong apparatus whose awareness does not extend beyond our sense-based knowledge. Bion explains:

> It is impossible to know reality for the same reason that makes it impossible to sing potatoes; they may be grown, or pulled, or eaten, but not sung.
> (Bion, 1965, p. 148)

Bion suggests that it is nonsensical to believe we can *know* this level of reality with the same sense-based mind that informs our knowledge of the physical world. We can only *be* it, or *become* it through intuitive means, and through this at-one-ment with an experience of ultimate reality (O), which is made possible only if we can bypass our logical minds. At the point at which the analyst has to transform the intuited truth into an interpretation, something will always be lost in translation, for in that gap between being and knowing, we convert that experience into words, into something that can be logically known.

It requires that difficult discipline of suspending memory, desire and understanding which, according to Bion, and *The Bhagavadgita*, is the mystical state. Although the aim of eschewing memories of the past and future desires in order to be more fully in the present, Bion (1970) pointed out, "A bad memory is not enough: what is ordinarily called forgetting is as bad as remembering" (p. 41). Á propos of this, people have sometimes asked me at lectures, "How can an analyst work without memory? How would you even recognize the patient, or remember what they said the session before?" This is obviously, or maybe *not* so obviously, far too literal an interpretation, for Bion was certainly not talking about having dementia or a lobotomy, but about a *temporary suspension* of memory that can minimize the distractions of everyday reality to maximize contact with the intuitive, dreaming mind. Since one is also still awake, one can later make use of whatever is gleaned from that waking dream, and so may spontaneously remember whatever relevant factors previously occurred, and how it might relate to the current moment. This is quite different than *trying to remember.* Like Rumi's idea that one cannot search for the "Friend," it is the difference between searching for a memory of something you once knew, using one's logical mind, and simply keeping that dreaming mind open, so that any thought or relevant memory might arise naturally in one's mind. This is in line with Heidegger's (1975) statement, "We never go to thoughts, thoughts come to us" (p. 6). Like Bion's "wild thoughts" or "thoughts without a thinker" (1978), if one trusts in the truth, it may come to mind. Whether in psychoanalytic work or any other creative work, one's memory is not fully lost, for the waking part of the mind is still intact, working *in conjunction with* the dreaming mind. The following example might help to illustrate these ideas.

Clinical example – "Ellie"

Ellie's mother was child-like and narcissistic, and often unavailable to her daughter emotionally. Ellie recently dreamt:

> I was swimming in a pond with my mother, it was like a pond near her childhood home which I didn't like swimming in because it seemed dirty. I took off my goggles and cleaned them, then put them back on. I decided to swim ahead of my mother so she could go at her own pace. I looked back at her once. I kept going, and I felt okay about it.... If anything had happened I probably couldn't have saved her anyway, I'm not that strong a swimmer.

Her last statement did not fit with the impression I'd gotten of Ellie as quite a good swimmer. When I mentioned this, Ellie agreed, somewhat perplexed, saying, "I don't know why I said that, I *am* a good swimmer. I mean I'm not a lifeguard or anything but I could get her back to shore if I needed to."

This discrepancy seemed significant, as were several noteworthy changes in her feelings about her mother that she described in this session. As a child she felt attuned to her mother, devoting herself to tending to her. And yet in this dream, for the first time, she *left her mother behind* to fend for herself. I thought this idea was the selected fact in this session, which provided the key to the dream. There was no longer any hope of fixing it. As Ellie grew increasingly aware of her own needs, she grieved the loss of her belief that her mother would ever get better, but this led to increasingly comforting boundaries between her and her mother, for she no longer needed the fantasy of someday fixing that relationship.

I interpreted that these changes followed on yesterday's dream in which Ellie seemed to feel unusually connected to me. She replied, "I never really had any-one who understood me." While she is afraid of getting hurt again if she allows these vulnerable feelings, today's dream nonetheless shows that an experience of a connection with me better allows her to see that what she had with her psy-chotic mother was not a connection at all, for she had buried all her real needs. She now realized that she did all she could, and yet you couldn't save her mother, not because she is a bad swimmer but because it was never possible to save her.

I felt strongly that this was a birth dream, which often goes along with sig-nificant changes, and she was dreaming of what it was like to have been in this polluted "womb" with an anxious and depressed mother all her life. She had assumed that her mother's illness was her fault, as if she were just "a bad swim-mer," a bad fetus. The memory of Ellie's connection to me in yesterday's dream was reflected in today's dream, for by "cleaning her goggles," she could now see "underwater" into these deeply unconscious feelings about that pre-natal "dirty pond," an amniotic fluid polluted by her mother's confusion, anxiety and depres-sion. Ellie has begun to swim far ahead of her sick mother to whom she had been tethered all her life.

Fairbairn's structural theory

Each child's capacity to develop her own mind, capable of real connections and separateness, has to resolve and move past these early defenses, identifications and idealizations of the parent who, in one way or other has failed the child. Fairbairn's ideas about the internalization of bad objects, alluded to in this chapter (above, p. 61) is relevant here.

> In my opinion, it is always 'bad objects' that are internalised in the first instance, since it is difficult to find any adequate motive for the internalisation of objects which are satisfying and 'good'... it is only insofar as his mother's breast fails

to satisfy his physical and emotional needs and thus becomes a bad object that it becomes necessary for the infant to internalise.

(Fairbairn, 1944, p. 93, fn. 1)

He adds that it is only these bad internalized objects that give rise to the internalization of what *seem* like "good" objects, but are in fact the defenses against the already internalized bad objects. Fairbairn's (1946) structural theory of the mind proposes a very different, more unified mind than one filled with these splintered aspects of parents. He writes:

I have come to adopt the principle of dynamic structure, in terms of which both structure divorced from energy and energy divorced from structure are meaningless concepts.

(Fairbairn, 1946, p. 149)

In his view of the mind, mental energy and mental structure cannot be separated, and I think this unified mind also reflects several of Bion's theories. Bion talked about the seemingly opposite functions of container and contained (the container of the mind and its contents), that are in fact in a constantly oscillating relationship with each other. Fairbairn's idea of structure and energy seem to reflect similarly opposing functions that in fact must act as one if the mind is to be an integrated whole. O also reflects the capacity for an integrated mind, but if the natural energy of the mind becomes bound up with the good *or* bad parental objects, as we see in Ellie, it deprives the child's mental energy of the inherent freedom to experience its own feelings. This idea of an integrated mind transcends a false self dominated by old internalizations, a mind capable of access to the energy of its own feeling, and the awe, of its own godhood.

For the many infants who never resolved the struggle to develop that unified mind or self, analysis serves as a battleground to have that fight for one's own mind. It may have previously taken the form of a religious battle, when religion, rather than psychology, was the guardian of morality and the immortal soul. In either case, Arjuna's war, and each of our individual wars, is also reflected in what Jesus describes as his purpose.

Do not think that I have come to bring peace to the world, I have not come to bring peace, but a sword. I have come to set a man against his father, a daughter against her mother, a daughter-in-law against her mother-in-law. One's enemies will be the members of one's own household.

(Jerusalem Bible, Matthew 10: 34–36)

Psychoanalysts are still dealing with the same internal challenges delineated thousands of years ago – the problems of individuation and the development of an authentic self or mind. In each case this requires the often violent pain of separation from parents who may have helped the child physically to thrive, but for various reasons, or their own problems of emotional development, may have been unable to help the child develop mentally. Given Bion's ideas about how the mind develops, this was not then, and is not now, an easy task for the parents or the child. Psychoanalysis is uniquely positioned for this fight, however, but only with the recognition that it is not one's ego, but one's eternal self/soul/mind that is battling to be free. As with Arjuna, the experience is one of being asked to "kill" the internalized parents with whom one may consciouisly and unconsciously be aligned, in order to achieve one's own mind. Although religion may for centuries have been the principal means of trying to make sense of the human condition, like most institutions, its own ideological rigidity often made it unsuitable to help in resolving this issue, once it was derailed from its pure search for knowledge. It needed prophets like Christ or Krishna, to remind them of the complexities of this internal battle against one's own loved ones, and their imagoes in one's mind.

The difficulties inherent in this are understandable in terms of Bion's (1965) ideas about the fear of, and resistance to, change, which makes change seem like a "catastrophic... subversion of the order or system" (p. 8). Without change, however, one may lose access to that primal realm of the spirit to which Krishna introduced Arjuna. In psychoanalytic terms, one must be willing to endure the "controlled breakdown" that is psychoanalysis, or risk losing access to essential Truth – O (p. 8).

Christ's message above is a recognition of the ultimate importance of spiritual Truth, of greater importance even than one's family, *if one's family is not aligned with Truth*. In the realm of absolute Truth, love can exist only in the presence of the love of Truth, and in its absence, the battles within one's family can be fierce.

Summary

Historically, there is a great deal of overlap between religion, mysticism and poetry, in the view of poets as divine conduits. Like Plato's (37 B.C.E.) idea, mentioned in Chapter 1, "Poets are nothing but interpreters of the gods" (p. 220), and it is true in the visual arts as well. The subject matter of much early Christian, Byzantine, Medieval and Renaissance paintings and sculptures was most essentially sacred art that was used for religious worship and the illumination of spiritual ideas. Again, before psychology, religious figures, poets and philosophers were keepers of the flame for the subtle examinations of mental life, morality and consciousness. Genesis, for instance, is really the genesis of consciousness – the challenges set out by tasting the fruits of the Tree of Knowledge of Good and Evil (knowledge of morality), and the Tree of Life (knowledge of mortality and divine immortality of the soul). But the "fruits" of these trees, namely good and evil, morality, mortality and immortality, were forbidden by God. It can be tricky to figure out which God represented this obstruction to the mind's capacity for higher knowledge, an obstruction to the natural human aspirations for our own divinity. Was it God or the Godhead?

There does seem to be an assumption of this obstructive God in some of the negative reactions attributed to the concept of O. Having written elsewhere about the source of this prohibitive God, I will not repeat it here, except to point out what I found to be a vast chasm and fundamental confusion between the primitive conscience of a punishing superego, and what we believe to be a more evolved conscience meant to unlock, rather than obstruct, the door to deeper spiritual knowledge. Unfortunately, the former seems to be more prevalent, and widely mistaken for the latter, which we *believe* to be a conscience, but seems as yet not nearly as developed as we would hope (cf. Reiner, 2009).

One thing seems clear however, these mystical or visionary perspectives are persistent over time, and are as much a mainstay of science as religion or the Arts. Although we've looked at the works of overtly mystical poets like Blake, Rumi, Kabir and Hafiz, these states of mind are central to the work of more secular poets as well. Emily Dickinson is not strictly thought of as a religious poet, but her work inhabits that divine, metaphysical, infinite realm characterized by O.

> *We never know how high we are*
> *Till we are called to rise;*
> *And then, if we are true to plan,*
> *Our statures touch the skies.*
>   (Dickinson, 2003, pp. 56–57)

She seems here to muse upon the measure of that mystical realm, about whose presence in our lives we know very little, a sort of calling that is essentially out of our hands. This unpredictable presence in one's life, while fearsome, seems to elevate one's existence. Her poems reflect these profound truths, that are synonymous with love. Many words in her poems are often represented in upper case letters – Love, Truth, Soul, Death, Sky – to suggest words that hold a different and more elevated meaning, a divine meaning, set apart from our prosaic everyday language using the same words. Even words like Sense, Madness, Delight and Brain are given this treatment, to suggest the broad, infinite meaning she is trying to embody. In this last poem, she again tries to find the measure of this aspect of the mind that underlies and suffuses her poems.

> *The Brain – is wider than the Sky –*
> *For – put them side by side –*
> *The one the other will contain*
> *With ease – and You – beside...*
>   (Dickinson, 1896, p. 51)

In Bion's terms, it is the infinite mind, O, that is wider than the brain, with which it is often confused. Unlike the electromagnetic and chemical functions of the body and brain, the mind or self, or character or spirit, is immeasurable, able, at least at times, to contain the universe, yet with no precise way of knowing what it contains. For such a challenge, perhaps we have to elevate our sights, and yet lower our expectations of reaching them, except through these imprecise measures of a poem or a dream.

References

The Bhagavadgita. (1979). In K. Bolle (Trans.). *The Bhagavadgita*. Berkeley and Los Angeles: University of California Press.

Bion, W. R. (1962). *Learning from Experience*. New York: Basic Books

Bion, W. R. (1963). *Elements of Psycho-Analysis*. New York: Basic Books.

Bion, W. R. (1965). Transformations. In *Seven Servants* (pp. 1–183). New York: Jason Aronson, 1977.

Bion, W. R. (1967b). Notes on memory and desire. *The Psychoanalytic Forum*, 2: 272–273; 279–290.

Bion, W. R. (1970). *Attention and Interpretation*. London: Karnac.

Bion, W. R. (1974). *Bion's Brazilian Lectures I: Sao Paulo, 1973*. Rio de Janeiro: Imago Editora LTDA.

Bion, W. R. (1977). 28 May 1977. In F. Bion (Ed.). *Taming Wild Thoughts* (pp. 27–38). London: Karnac Books, 1997.

Bion, W. R. (1978). *Four Discussion with W. R. Bion*. Perthshire: Cluny Press.

Bion, W. R. (1989). The grid. In *Two Papers: The Grid and Caesura* (pp. 1–33). London: Karnac.

Blake, W. (1790–93). The marriage of heaven and hell. (Plate 14). In M. H. Abrams (Ed.). *The Norton Anthology of English Literature, Fourth Edition*, Volume 2, (Plate 14, p. 56). New York, London: W. W. Norton & Company, 1979.

Dickinson, E. (1890). Much madness is divinest sense. In R. Ellman; R. O'Clair (Eds.). *The Norton Anthology of Modern Poetry, Second Edition* (p. 38). New York, London: W.W. Norton & Company, 1973.

Dickinson, E. (1896). The brain—Is wider than the sky. In R. Ellman; R. O'Clair (Eds.). *The Norton Anthology of Modern Poetry, Second Edition* (pp. 39–40). New York, London: W.W. Norton & Company, 1973.

Dickinson, E. (2003). Poem XCVII. In G. Stade (Editorial Director). *The Collected Poems of Emily Dickinson*. New York: Barnes & Noble Classics.

Eckhart, M. (1941). In R. B. Blakney (Trans.). *Meister Eckhart: A Modern Translation*. New York: Harper Torch/Harper & Row.

Eckhart, M. (1994). Sermon 22. In O. Davies (Trans.). *Meister Eckhart: Selected Writings*. New York, London: Penguin Books.

Einstein, A. (1952). In L. Barnett, (Ed.). *The Universe and Dr. Einstein* (p. 117). New York, A Mentor Book, The New American Library.

Einstein, A. (1950). *Out of My Later Years*. New York: Philosophical Library.

Einstein, A. (1954). *Ideas and Opinions*. New York: Dell Publishing Company.

Exodus 3: 14. (1968). In *The Jerusalem Bible,* Reader's Edition. New York: Doubleday & Company, Inc..

Fairbairn, W. R. D. (1944). Endopsychic structure considered in terms of object-relations. In *An Object Relations Theory of the Personality* (pp. 82–136). New York: Basic Books, 1952.

Fairbairn, W. R. D. (1946). Object-relationships and dynamic structure. In *An Object Relations Theory of the Personality* (pp. 137–151). New York: Basic Books, 1952.

Freud, S. (1916). Letter to Lou Andrea-Salome. In E. Freud (Ed.). *Letters of Sigmund Freud*. New York: Basic Books.

Freud, S. (1927). *The Future of an Illusion, Standard Edition*, 21 (pp. 3–56). London: Hogarth Press.

Freud, S. (1930). *Civilization and Its Discontents, Standard Edition*, 21 (pp. 59–14). London: Hogarth Press.

Grotstein, J. (2007). *A Beam of Intense Darkness: Wilfred Bion's Legacy to Psychoanalysis*. London: Karnac.

Hafiz. (2006). In D. Ladinsky (Trans.). *I Heard God Laughing: Poems of Hope and Joy*. London: Penguin Books.

Hafiz. (2011). In D. Ladinsky (Trans.). *A Year with Hafiz: Daily Contemplations*. London: Penguin Books.

Heidegger, M. (1927). Being and time. In J. Stambaugh (Trans.). Albany, NY: State University of New York Press, 1996.

Heidegger, M. (1975). *Poetry, Language, Thought*. New York: Harper & Row.

Gospel of Matthew 5:17. (1968). *Jerusalem Bible, Reader's Edition*. New York: Doubleday & Company, Inc., 1968.

Jung, C. G. (1935). *Analytical Psychology: Its Theory & Practice. Lecture One* (pp. 3–25). New York: Random House, Vintage Books.

Keats, J. (1817). Letter to George and Tom Keats. In P. De Man (Ed.). *The Selected Poetry of Keats*. New York: New American Library, Signet Classical Poetry Series, 1966.

Klein, M. (1937). Love, guilt and reparation. In *The Writings of Melanie Klein*, Volume 1 (pp. 306–343). London: Hogarth Press and the Institute of Psycho-Analysis, 1975.

Klein, M. (1946). Notes on some schizoid mechanisms. In *Envy and Gratitude, and Other Works, 1946–1963* (pp. 1–24). New York: Delacorte Press/Seymour Lawrence, 1975.

Milton, J. (1650). Sonnet on his blindness. In J. S. Smart (Ed.). *The Sonnets of Milton*. Glasgow: Maclehose, Jackson and Co (Glasgow University Publishers), 1921.

Milton, J. (1667). Paradise Lost, Book 3. In *Paradise Lost and Paradise Regained* (pp.62–81). New York: Airmont Publishing Co.,1968.

Nietzsche, F. (1887). The Gay Science. In W. Kaufmann (Trans.). New York: Vintage Books/ Random House, 1974.

Pagels, E. (1979). *The Gnostic Gospels*. New York: Vintage Books.

Pagels, E. (1989). *The Gnostic Gospels*. New York: Vintage Books.

Pessoa, F. (1931). *The Book of Disquiet*. In A. Mac Adam (Trans.). Boston, MA: Exact Change/ Pantheon Books, a division of Random House, 1998.

Reiner, A. (2009). *The Quest for Conscience and the Birth of the Mind*. London: Karnac.

Reiner, A. (2022). *W.R. Bion's Theories of Mind: A Contemporary Introduction*. London: Routledge.

Reiner, A. (2023). Boddhisatva gets the news. Unpublished.

Rumi. (1981). *The Ruins of the Heart*. In E. Helminski (Trans.) (pp. 36–38). Putney, VT: Threshold Books.

Rumi. (1984). In J. Moyne; C. Barks (Trans.). *Open Secret: Versions of Rumi*. Putney, VT: Threshold Books.

Rumi (1993). *Love is a Stranger*. In K. Helminski (Trans.). Putney, VT: Threshold Books.

Rumi (1994). In W. M. Thackston, Jr. (Trans.). *Signs of the Unseen: Discourses of Jalalludin Rumi*. Putney, VT: Threshold Books.

Segal, H. (1981). Notes on symbol formation. In *The Work of Hannah Segal: A Kleinian Approach to Clinical Practice* (pp. 49–68). New York: Jason Aronson.

Thackston, Jr., W. M. (1994). (Trans.) Introduction. In *Signs of the Unseen: The Discourses of Jalaluddin Rumi* (pp. vii–xxvi). Putney, VT: Threshold Books.

Winnicott, D. W. (1960). Ego distortion in terms of the true and false self. In M. Masud R. Khan (Ed.), *Maturational Processes and the Facilitating Environment* (pp. 140–152). London, New York: Karnac, 1965.

Chapter 4

Omnia mutantur (all things change)

Ode To O

There is a Woman in this room you cannot see.
No, not me.
She is the future coming soon
though how can the future be in this room
except by a trick of sub-atomic sleight-of-hand
which even the quantum physicists can't understand.
But I can feel her
whom I am becoming at this and every moment
disappearing like a quark
only to show up over there
in the past,
which was me,
now lying like a sloughed off skin,
while the Woman alive in transitional being,
still broken into my component parts,
but no cause for alarm,
it's just Me = mc2-
now you see me, now you don't...
me neither...
Oh oh... O.

(Reiner, 2008b, p. 11)

This poem clearly diverges from any of the logical meanings ascribed to Bion's concept of O.

In this chapter, we will look further at the experience of O through poets, Fernando Pessoa and Paul Valery, as well as some of my poems. Since O is by definition "unknown and unknowable," this metaphysical, fundamentally nonrational reality may be better represented by poetic, visual, musical, and scientific languages. While I did not set out to do that in the poem above, it seems to have

DOI: 10.4324/9781003470953-5

emerged anyway to try to convey something of the feeling of that ephemeral, enig-matic and constantly changing elusive reality in ourselves and our environment.

Music "speaks" to us beyond words, and although poems do use words, they use them in a different way, not just for their lexical meanings, but for the musi-cality of the words – their rhythms, rhymes and alliterative patterns. However, it is a language of inherent uncertainty, since neither music nor poetry can provide clear or demonstrative explanations of what is being expressed. We feel something from music without necessarily knowing why. The content of a poem is conveyed through both the feelings evoked by its "music," and its verbal meaning, working together in ways that cannot completely be distinguished from each other.

In my poem above, even attempting to express the inexpressible O implies a belief that such an unknowable and unprovable reality exists, despite its slippery nature, and further implies that there is a means for the human mind to apprehend it. This uncertainty of that ultimately unknowable esoteric knowledge is reflected both in the content and the form of the poem. Ideas of inherent uncertainty and constant change will be examined in this chapter through science, philosophy and poetry.

Quantum physics and the mind as invisible mysteries

The paradoxical world of subatomic physics is evoked in "Ode To O" as a meta-phor for the paradoxical mental states in our ever-shifting minds. Although my understanding of modern physics is minimal at best, I thought I would say a little of what I do know of that quantum realm as it is reflected in the poem. The discovery in quantum physics that a photon – a particle of light – can at times behave as a particle and at times as a wave, seemed to me to have at least a metaphorical simi-larity to our bicameral minds that also function in fundamentally different ways on conscious and unconscious levels. One might say, again metaphorically, that the mind sometimes takes on a more organized function, acting like a specific particle, and sometimes acts like the amorphous emotional waves of the infant's primitive oceanic feeling. While quantum physics attempts to describe an elusive *physical* world of energy and particles that is invisible to the naked eye, the focus of psy-choanalysts is on an equally elusive and invisible *metaphysical* world of psychic reality, which includes the dream-like functioning of O.

There is also the phenomenon of "quantum entanglement," or "entangled photon pairs." This peculiar phenomenon occurs when one member of a proton pair, when separated from the other, is given some kind of stimulus, causing the other member of the pair to behave in exactly the same way as the first, even when they are separated by huge distances. Recent experiments by Chinese scientists provided proof of these events and found that the behavior of a photon pair separated from each other by 1,500 miles were perfectly correlated to each other (Netburn, 2017). The speed limits of these particles at their lowest levels were at least 10,000 times faster than light.

A great controversy existed between Bohr and Einstein on this matter. Einstein found these results disturbing, calling it, "ghostly action at a distance," and in a paper by Einstein, Podolsky, and Rosen, stated, "No reasonable definition of reality could be expected to permit this" (Talbot, 1988, p. 31). Despite Einstein's efforts to disprove it, the debate raged on for decades, with one experiment showing that information like this can be passed between particles at over seven and a half times the speed of light (Talbot, 1988, p. 35).

There are metaphorical similarities to the phenomena of profound inexplicable intuitions like the prophetic dream described in Chapter 1. However, we can also see evidence of this in more familiar psychoanalytic theories like projective iden-tification, the mother's uncanny ability to receive information from the nonverbal infant, or in the analyst's ability to receive information from the patient. According to Bion (1962), projective identification is associated with the mother's capacity for "reverie," but it is never specified how this works, nor can it be, for it belongs in this vaguely dream-like state, beyond rational data. Like the behavior of those pho-ton pairs, thoughts exist in fields of energy where communications can be transmit-ted and received, although we do not know how, but it is in the state of "becoming one with the other," that Bion associates with O.

Likewise, projections of patients' states of mind into the analyst that can be sent and received at unconscious levels which might also be said to take place at a "ghostly" or "voodoo" level, transmissions of thoughts and feelings that, like photons, have no mass. Although physicists cannot explain these perfect correla-tions of separated photon pairs, they do seem to exist, as do these uncanny, and also unexplained, mental communications. I think we can also say that, as with photons, the mental illuminations of absolute truth have no charge, for they are neither posi-tive nor negative, good nor bad, they just are. Bion's statement that O is nonhuman reflects the idea that these truths carry no human judgment. Like "thoughts without a thinker," they are truths that exist whether or not we human beings think them, whether or not we approve of them.

While these kinds of occult phenomena have traditionally been ignored in psy-choanalysis, Freud's relationship to the occult was ambivalent. Despite his interest in uncanny phenomena like clairvoyance and telepathy, he feared that such sub-jects would tarnish the scientific reputation of psychoanalysis. He warned Ferenczi against publishing his paper about esoteric matters as it would be like "throwing a bomb into the psychoanalytic house" (Jones, 1957, p. 393). As noted in Chapter 1, Ferenczi's idea of the "astra" reflected upon this uncanny level of experience that sometimes develops in patients who have experienced early birth traumas or emo-tional neglect by physically or mentally absent mothers (cf. Reiner, 2017). Bion's idea of O, and of the mystical intuitive communications that are sensed but cannot be explained, brings that level of inexplicable mental phenomena to center stage in psychoanalytic work.

Metaphysical uncertainties of an unmanifest psychic realm, and the physical uncertainties of quantum physics have been compared by many scientists and phi-losophers to reveal these kinds of inexplicable mysteries that speak to the limita-tions of our knowledge in both realms.

Buddhist Impermanence and Bion's "catastrophic change"

Omnia mutantur is Latin meaning "All things change." Change is an essential and unavoidable fact of life, and an unavoidable tenet of Buddhist philosophy, which views the central factor in the suffering of mankind is our fear of change and our inability to accept it. We human beings seem to try endlessly to escape these facts, not necessarily consciously, and yet the simple facts of aging, growing old and dying, which no one escapes, seem to be beyond our capacity to tolerate. We are not like roses that blossom one day into a glorious and colorful flower, only to die a brutal death as their petals pale and weaken and fall to the ground, leaving an unimpressive spindly stem. What they don't have are mirrors to record their downfall, while we humans notice the signs in our faces, the sagging skin, the loss of vitality and color that signal to us the end. Everyone and everything dies, but we are the only ones who complain about it every step of the way.

This is no simple matter, nor is it mere vanity. For we humans are no fan of new ideas that will change something less obvious than our faces or bodies, our minds. And so, as discussed, the generator of new ideas – the mystic or genius – then becomes a lightning rod for fear. Bion's (1965) idea of the catastrophic nature of change, briefly discussed in the last chapter, is problematic in a field like psychoanalysis in which change is an underlying aim, but is experienced as a mental crisis.

> [Change] is catastrophic in that it is accompanied by feelings of disaster in the participants; it is catastrophic in the sense that it is sudden and violent in an almost physical way.
>
> (Bion, 1965, p. 8)

This is not intellectual change, but change that threatens the core of one's existence. But if change itself feels catastrophic, the apparent simplicity of Buddha's formula for a peaceful mind is belied by how enormously disturbing, and unacceptable, we find change to be.

The continuous transformations in my poem, "Ode To O," reflect that dynamic quality of psychic life, just as light can manifest either as waves and particles, or energy and matter are constantly being transformed. Our minds are in constant oscillations between conscious and unconscious modalities, unpredictable changeability that generates great fear in people about this enigmatic realm of a mental, emotional life beyond our control. Our own feelings may be beyond our conscious understanding and rational control.

Knowing what we know about primitive infantile mental life, we can see why people early on become frightened of change, even in the natural order of life. What we are really afraid of, however, is our own minds, that which remains unknown, or is associated with frightening aspects of past experiences.

One otherwise independent patient recently began to experience intense anxiety when she became aware of the infantile feelings of unmet needs in her emotionally detached mother, and also of her rage at this frustrating mother. While we had worked toward this during the two years of her analysis at that point, she was no longer just *thinking about* it, but was *feeling* it. This, of course, included the level of anxiety and anger of her infant self, a kind of experiential change that cuts to the heart of one's existence, an emotional change that can no longer be denied.

While we human beings find the impermanence of our own lives painful, even in these moment-to-moment emotional shifts, failing to accept the reality of impermanence in the face of our unavoidable experiences of birth, life and death, is essentially an aversion to reality, truth and growth. It is a denial, really, of life. Avoiding the reality of death thereby creates a kind of mental death.

Any real emotional progress gives rise to fears about the sequelae of change, the fear of becoming a different person whom one does not know, without their time-tested defenses of splitting, denial and dissociation. This is one of the reasons that psychoanalysis has to proceed slowly, for each significant gain is felt as a loss, and each of those perceived losses have to be mentally processed and mourned. The catastrophe of change reflects a fear that one's old beliefs, which are indistinguishable from one's self, will be lost or destroyed in the process of learning. In a very real sense this is true. The birth of a baby, for example, is the end, or "death" of the fetus, who is now replaced by a neonatal infant forced to adapt to a new reality, who must learn to breathe in a new gaseous environment, and is subject to strange and uncomfortable experiences of cold, hunger and a separate existence, which the fetus was protected from in the womb. The discomforts inherent in the natural impermanence of life are unavoidable, for without being born, the life of the fetus would eventually end in actual death, both for the fetus and the infant. But each of our later, and constant transformations into new versions of our physical and mental selves can be similarly terrifying. How frightening these will be is to some extent dictated by the relative safety or danger of those early experiences, and so we are not doomed to misery merely on the grounds of being born, but by whether or not the inherent discomforts and anxieties are mitigated by the care of a sentient presence able to protect our emotional and mental growth.

The dangers of O

The fear of change is dictated in large part by an outcome that is unknown and unknowable, not knowing if one's mind can withstand the change. However, the new idea may reflect an old feeling that was too dangerous to feel or think, or happened before one had a mind able to think. In this case, the fear of the future is really an unremembered memory of the past, as Winnicott (1974) put forth in his idea of the infant's "fear of breakdown" (p. 105). Such experiences cannot be remembered because there was no mind yet available to feel it. Therefore, they continue to exist in a kind of mental purgatory, neither here nor there, in a mind that does not yet exist. The danger one feels in any attempt to make that past known is real.

Enlightenment and mental transcendence can be dangerous, and navigating the dream-like boundaryless world of the unconscious without losing one's bearings is challenging. While Bion (1970), said that at-one-ment with O is facilitated by "disciplined denial of memory and desire" (p. 41), one cannot suspend the memory of unremembered memories. And so Bion also pointed out that emptying the mind of those ego functions can lead to the feelings of ego-regression, and yet this is what we experience with our patients in every session if we are to find them in that vast, expansive mental universe. Do we dare to go there, to admit to ourselves that we do not know our way, armed only with the hope that we might find it anyway.

Something to Do with O (But Who Knows)

The meaning of a poem
is the poem.
Is-ness is my business,
which only the poem knows.
All the rest is unmanifest,
like some kind of esoteric test
we are bound to fail –
unless failure is success –
or what is worse,
unless a blessing is a curse.
The real answers, while not exactly hidden
are not exactly forbidden,
nor are they exactly square or round
or any other shape that has ever been found.
But where 'O' where are we supposed to meet,
you and me, each in his own galaxy,
in minds undefined and still unnamed,
playing Peek-a-Boo, though this is no game.
Peek-a-boo! I cannot see you
or your elusive Universal Truth.
I try not to care, but it seems so unfair,
because somehow I know you're there.
                    (Reiner, 2022, unpublished)

In the ancient Greek myth, Icarus and his father were imprisoned by the King. His father managed, however, to create wings of wax so that he and his son could escape, but Icarus, failing to heed his father's warning, flew too close to the sun, where his wings melted, and he was plunged into the sea and drowned. Access to the waking dream state of O fuels creativity, and can be a welcomed escape from the imprisonment of our quotidian, prosaic, finite minds, but one does have to be prepared for such a journey. One's "wings" need to be strong enough to keep one aloft, with a mind sufficiently strong to navigate the storms and gales of one's most primitive thought processes, in addition to those of the patient. This is the basis of Bion's (1970) warning to young analysts and therapists, discouraging them from trying to make contact with O, by suspending memory, desire and understanding, *unless* they have had their primitive paranoid-schizoid and depressive anxieties properly analyzed. Unless, that is, those memories have been retrieved. Experiencing a breakdown of the ego is essentially being plunged, like Icarus, into the unnavigable waters of one's own unconscious, where, unless contained by a mind that can tolerate those primitive feelings, one may drown.

This mythical escape reminded me of Bion's lament at the end of *The Dawn of Oblivion*, the third book of his fictionalized autobiography, *A Memoir of the Future*.

> All my life I have been imprisoned, frustrated, dogged by commonsense, reason, memories, desires and—greatest bugbear of all—understanding and being understood. This [book] is an attempt to express my rebellion, to say 'Good-bye' to all that.
>
> (Bion, 1979, Epilogue, p. 578)

A mind lacking contact with the infinite realm of dream and imagination can be a torturous prison, and Bion's need for mental freedom was clearly fierce. He speaks here of the need to escape the imprisoning ego that blocks mental freedom and creativity. His *Memoir of the Future* is essentially a stream of consciousness, or *un*consciousness, through which Bion sought that escape. He continued on to acknowledge that he had not succeeded in cleansing his book of the taint of common sense and reason, but he did attempt, like Icarus, to escape that imprisonment by soaring into the transcendent world of dreams while still awake.

Clinical vignette – Mrs. A

This clinical example shows the power of those unconscious winds. Mrs. A survived growing up with a depressed mother and absent father, but after years of analysis she was beginning to experience the pain and neglect she thought she had left behind. She had begun to realize the distance she felt from a husband who, like her father, was also emotionally detached. This dream laid bare some of her real feelings.

> I was leaving my husband and son, but I knew that once I was gone they would forget about me, as if I never existed. I knew I would miss my son, and wondered how I would deal with the grief. But I didn't really feel guilt for leaving because they wouldn't remember me. I went to a beautiful beach... it was almost like a postcard, **too** beautiful, too perfect. There were signs on the beach that warned of tsunamis, and police sirens were going off to warn people. But the grief. Where could I go to deal with that?

The too beautiful postcard of a beautiful beach represented the idealization of her mother. Convinced that she had saved her mother by being such a good mother to her, Mrs. A felt she had handled the pain of having no mother to care for her. With this dream, however, we see that this idealized loving mother/self was like the picture postcard beach in her dream, which like all idealized states, is "too beautiful." I thought her grief at leaving her children also represented her emotional self-exile from her parents, and from herself. Like the alarm going off on that beautiful beach, she was now being warned of a tsunami of painful feelings. A prolific imagination can convince children that the traumas they suffered are gone, when in fact they are buried beneath a beautiful, but fake picture.

In response to my interpretation Mrs. A said, "What's wrong with creating a beautiful reality? Doesn't everyone do that?" Her irritation with me was striking, and unusual, as she still idealizes herself, and sometimes our work, but this was real and intense irritation at me, as she felt I was threatening to rob her of love and beauty, and all she'd believed was good. She could not yet accept that her attempts to escape the pain of her reality using the flimsy "wings" of idealization, were doomed to failure.

Mrs. A left the session in anger, but the next day it was clear that she had heard me. She was thoughtful, fluctuating between depressive pain and the illusion of her perfect beauty. I thought her ability to be angry at me, and to doubt me, was a healthy reaction to a mother-me she could not trust, and by whom she could dare to feel disappointed. Such patients are stuck between their love of truth and loyalty and the defensive structure that had held their feelings of terror at bay. But despite her defenses, Mrs. A's desire for truth was quite strong. Those defenses are the wax wings upon which one may briefly soar, but never, ultimately to freedom. In giving up the beautiful old dream, one faces the danger of losing one's sense of self, and one's grip on what they thought was reality, and yet to avoid contact with the deeper aspects of the self-insures a kind of imprisonment by which one forfeits emotional life and stultifies growth.

Despite her effort to preserve her old "lie" of a beautiful mother/self, Mrs. A found her way back to her need for truth, and was able to think about what I said. I thought this spoke to her courage and her inherent love of truth. While I was surprised that my interpretation elicited such intense anger, it had clearly touched a very old nerve, and had challenged her belief that she could rewrite reality and make a beautiful picture for herself. Over the next few sessions, this led to the beginning of a new relationship to truth, and a new relationship with me as someone who, despite the pain I caused her, was felt as helping to find a new truth.

Fernando Pessoa

The kind of dilemma Mrs. A faced is certainly an issue in the works of Fernando Pessoa. This early 20th century Portuguese poet was a unique personality, or I should say, "personalities," for in at least one book he wrote from the perspectives of different characters, each with his own name and personality. His book of poems, *Fernando Pessoa & Co.* refers to these different personalities housed within his mind (Zenith, 1998). One poet in the book is named, "Álvaro de Campos," and described as a "jaded sensationalist" (Zenith, 1998, p. 141), while "Richard Reis" is a "sad epicurean" whose poetry "was not of this world" (Zenith, 1998, p. 93). Many of them, however, address similar existential experiences of being, often found in his work. In one voice of Álvaro de Campos, Pessoa writes of becoming one with whatever he loves or for which he feels a kinship. This is part of that feeling, mentioned above (Chapter 3), in which Pessoa delights in "losing himself," in writing without thinking, using words "without meaning, softly flowing, in a fluidity of felt water..." (Pessoa, 1931, p. 9). It is not that these words are actually meaningless, except perhaps in the sense that dream language may *seem* meaningless because we do not know its meaning through typically rational channels. But losing himself in his external daydreams is very much what Bion suggests for the psychoanalyst, to facilitate the "kinship" or oneness with the patient, through that waking dream state of O.

This immersion in "being," like Bion's idea of a mind without memory and desire, is reflected in the following excerpt of a poem by Pessoa.

> *I feel at each moment that I've just been born*
> *Into a completely new world...*
> *I have no philosophy, I have senses...*
> *If I speak of Nature it's not because I know what it is*
> *But because I love it...*
> *To love is innocence,*
> *And the sum of innocence is not to think...*
> (Pessoa, 1914, pp. 11–12)

From this point of view, Being – or having a self or mind – could paradoxically be seen as *not* Being, at least in the usual sense of one's known ego, for here one has "no philosophy, no senses," and no thinking. The analyst's apprehension of O in a session requires this same experience of leaving rational thinking behind by training one's mind to suspend memory (thoughts of the past), desire, (hopes for the future), and all knowledge that superficially organizes our understanding. All of these ego functions obstruct the unfettered experience of someone just born, where one has only the present moment, a moment that has never happened before and so cannot fit into any theory, it is pure experience. Although Pessoa compares it to a newborn, it is a newborn who "... noticed [he] had really and truly been born" (Pessoa, 1914, p. 11). This reflects the idea of a relationship between conscious and unconscious states, as Bion (1970) put it, between primal paranoid-schizoid and depressive anxieties (Ps] D), a relationship between that infant state *and* the more evolved awareness of a more developed mind.

Pessoa constantly crossed fluid lines of conscious and unconscious, and at times seemed truly to have lost himself, for it is not clear, at least to me, to what extent those different aspects of himself whom he presented as poets in their own right, reflect a fragmented self. Despite not knowing the details of Pessoa's self-described "fragmentation," the experience expressed in the poem above does not seem to be of someone psychotic, at least at that moment, for it masterfully describes what goes into that deeper mode of unconscious being and thinking. He raises important questions about the nature of reality and being, and of expanding our need to include the world of dreams in our experience. It is also important to note the dangers, as Bion did, of getting lost in that dream-like world without sufficient emotional development, which can lead to a pathological dissociation and ego regression. However, one might also get lost in a world of hypertrophied logic with insufficient access to one's dreams and emotions, like Bion's comment above about being "imprisoned" in reason and common sense.

Pessoa wonders about these states of mind, but is clearly familiar with the kind of nothingness and nonbeing that is really a deeper kind of being.

> This is my morality, or metaphysics, or me: Passerby of everything... belonging to nothing, desiring nothing, being nothing... I don't know if I'm happy this way. Nor do I care.
>
> (Pessoa, 1998, p. 1)

This may very well describe the idea of O, where judgments of good or bad are simply not relevant. Indeed, this next excerpt from one of his poems is a fair description of the experience of suspending memory, desire and knowledge.

> *What matters is to know how to see,*
> *To know how to see without thinking,*
> *To know how to see when seeing*
> *And not think when seeing*
> *Nor see when thinking.*
> *But this...*
> *This requires deep study.*
> *Lessons in unlearning....*
>
> (Pessoa, 1914, p. 57)

To be in the moment with no screen between you and the current reality, one has to "unlearn" and unclutter one's mind of what one already knows and believes. Pessoa's "lessons in unlearning" is in line with Bion's suggestion to analysts to forget our theories in order to experience each new reality for oneself.

In another poem, Pessoa addresses the immediacy of experiencing the world in this way where one does not *know*, but rather, one *Is*.

> *The only hidden meaning of things*
> *Is that they have no hidden meaning.*
> *It is the strangest thing of all,*
> *Stranger than all poets' dreams*
> *And all philosophers' thoughts,*
> *That things are really what they seem to be*
> *And there's nothing to understand.*
> *Yes, this is what my senses learned on their own:*
> *Things have no meaning; they exist.*
> *Things are the only hidden meaning of things.*
>
> (Pessoa, 1914, p. 62)

We don't know how closely Pessoa's experience bears witness to the experience as O, the thing-in-itself, but it is certainly part of Bion's idea of the importance of a logically unknowable O as the central psychoanalytic perspective. For Pessoa, the seemingly obvious "hidden" meaning here is the thing-in-itself, where things exist, and *we* exist, and although the thing-in-itself is not consciously knowable, it *is* us.

I think that Bion's desire to provide psychoanalysts with a book of poems specifically for them, may reflect his desire to provide this experience of "being" or "becoming" one's experience, beyond one's rational, finite self.

Paul Valéry

As we've seen, the words in a poem do not convey their meaning in the same way as everyday prosaic language. Like the symbols of a dream, it is a far more mysterious language, at least to our logical waking minds. Through symbols and metaphors, the language of the dreaming self provides a *feeling* of the message, not necessarily just in the words but in how those words sing and dance with each other. Most people are bewildered by dreams – their own and those of others – and perhaps also bewildered by poems that often yield from the same unconscious domain. Valéry's description of the difference between the languages of poetry and prose is probably the clearest one I have heard, expressed below in this very simple formula.

Poetry : Prose :: Dancing : Walking (or Running)

(Valéry, 1958, p. xv)

In plain language, poetry is to prose what dancing is to walking. Valéry explains that prose is instrumental, and like walking it has a logical purpose and an aim, namely, to get from point A to point B. Dance, on the other hand, has no such aim, for its essential aim is the dance itself, an expression of itself.

The dance is quite another matter. It is, of course, a system of actions... whose end is in themselves.

(Valéry, 1958, p. 70)

This is why poetry cannot be translated, because the words *are* the meaning, it is the thing-in-itself which cannot be known, but as Bion (1970) said of O, one can become it (p. 26). This describes a marriage of form and content, where the two are inseparable, for the content of a poem is contained and conveyed in the form, and its meaning is a product of that marriage. In these lines from a poem, Valéry says of the poet:

It is intelligence, vigilance, that gives birth to dream:
It is sleep that sees clearly...
It is the lack and the blank that create.
(Bion, 1970, p. 147)

The words in a poem are conveyed in the language of a dream, a language that every analyst needs to learn. This is true whether or not the patient has remembered a dream for the analyst to work with directly, for according to Bion the unconscious is always dreaming and it is the analyst's job to "read" that dream. Bion (1992) distinguishes Freud's idea of dreaming as pertaining to sleep, from his own view that a dream "…is the way [the mind] works when awake" (p. 43). Grotstein (2009) stressed this idea, and often mentioned, "Freud's injunction that the analytic session itself can be considered to be a dream" (p. 27). The analyst interprets the unconscious whether it is represented in an actual night-time dream or whether he hears the unconscious symbols embedded in the patient's seemingly conscious associations, random thoughts, feelings, gestures and general concerns.

Like a dream, the poem created in this way does not know what it is about, for it is not the words themselves in a poem that convey the meaning, but rather the *relationships* between the words, ideas, rhythms and musicality that give it meaning. And it is all created in the relationship between a mind that is half-asleep and half-awake. I will include two poems that reflect these ideas about a state of mind that is necessary for poets and artists, but also, according to Bion's idea of O, necessary for the psychoanalyst. The first is one that I wrote, and the second is an excerpt from a poem by Valéry.

Gravity

Gravity connects sun and moon to earth,
connecting moments of time
which fall together to make a life,
as letters fall together to make words
falling together to make perfect poems
by poets falling apart.
                    (Reiner, 2008a, p. 12)

Valéry writes:

In the poet:…
It is intelligence, vigilance, that gives birth to dream;
It is sleep that sees clearly;
It is the image and phantom that look;
It is the lack and the blank that create.
                    (Valéry, 1950, p. 147)

Again, one gives up one's mind in the service of access to that deeper mind of O, the empty mind that is capable of dreaming as a form of unconscious thinking. It is consistent with Valéry's conclusion here, about the poetic clarity of the sleeping mind, with its absence of conscious effort – "the lack and the blank." I think I was getting at the same idea with the sense of "poets falling apart," as one gives us the control of one's logical mind. Like writers and artists who have to face the dreaded "blank page" or "blank canvas," in order to engage the dream state of O. It requires both the mental relaxation of sleep and the heightened vigilance of wakefulness – the binocular view into the internal world of imagination and the external world of the physical senses.

> [T]he poetic state takes hold of us, develops, and finally disintegrates... This is to say that the state of poetry is completely irregular, inconstant, involuntary, and fragile, and that we lose it, as we find it, by accident.
>
> (Valéry, 1958, p. 60)

This is O – dreaming while awake – and a sense of unity in the mind. Valéry talked about this sense of unity in writing poetry, as well as that sense of unity that is imparted to those who read or hear it. I think this unity may be another reason why Bion was moved to publish a book of poems for psychoanalysts, for that sense of mental integration that it imparts, and from which it derives, is surely an aim, consciously or not, in the mind of the psychoanalyst and the analysand.

> If poetry affects someone, it is not by dividing him in his nature... Poetry must extend over the whole being... for poetry aims to arouse or reproduce the unity and harmony of the living person, an extraordinary unity that shows itself when a man is possessed by an intense feeling that leaves none of his powers disengaged.
>
> (Valéry, 1958, p. 211)

This is a bold and lofty goal, engaging the same sense of harmony and integration that underlies access to O. It is also essential to Bion's idea about the oscillating relationship between Ps]D that, according to Bion, is necessary in fashioning an interpretation. Bion here uses Klein's language of her theory about the transition from the primitive paranoid-schizoid position (Ps) to the depressive position (D), but he uses these terms differently. He is first of all using it clinically, as a means of describing a transition from what he calls "patience to security." The analyst requires "patience," he says, to tolerate the primitive anxieties and disorganization of the paranoid-schizoid position that are evoked in each session with the patient, until the analyst achieves a state "security," that comes as he or she reaches a sense of understanding, and the diminished anxiety and organization characteristic of the depressive position. The following statement would be Bion's version of the unity and harmony described by Valéry.

> I consider that no analyst is entitled to believe that he has done the work required to give an interpretation unless he has passed through both phases – 'patience' and security'.
>
> (Bion, 1970, p. 124)

This occurs through what Valéry called the "vigilance" that gives birth to a dream. Security cannot be achieved through the analyst's imposition of theories he already knows, but only through a fresh awareness that comes of having tolerated not-know-ing. O is like the dream-like state that Valéry described as the "irregular, inconstant, involuntary" state of writing a poem. In both disciplines, mental unity consists of a marriage of opposites, the capacity to shift between two different states.

I think the widespread resistance to these difficult fluctuations through such dif-ferent and challenging states of mind accounts for why Bion's concept of O contin-ues to be controversial. Nonetheless, Bion continues to stress its importance as the central psychoanalytic perspective.

> The success of analysis depends on the maintenance of a psychoanalytic point of view... the psychoanalytic vertex is O.
>
> (Bion, 1970, p. 27)

Part of the controversy has to do with the difficulties inherent in grasping and describing the indescribable. Like poetry, the reality to which O approximates inevitably gets lost in translation, as both poet and analyst engage in a struggle to express that which is written between the lines.

The dual mental functions of the dreaming and waking mind are beautifully expressed in these last two poetic prose statements by Valéry.

> A poem must be a holiday of Mind...Holiday: it is a game, but solemn, ordered and significant...
>
> (Valéry, 1950, p. 147).

> Thought is hidden in verse like the nutritive virtue in fruit... One perceives only pleasure but one receives a substance. Enchantment veils this imperceptible nourishment it brings with it.
>
> (Valéry, 1950, p, 148)

Part of the effects of each of the Arts is to give pleasure, while often also imparting truth. As Valéry says, the poem's gift to the reader is a "holiday of Mind," a respite from the strictures of our overly logical egoistic minds, but this "enchantment" is accompanied by solemnity, significance, and mental nourishment. While pleasure is not viewed as the aim of psychoanalysis, which is often extremely painful, in the attendant solemnity, order, significance and truth it provides, both analyst and analysand may also discover the pleasure inherent in an experience of deep truth. This sense of pleasure derives from the power of truth to lead to freedom and men-tal development. As Christ said to his followers:

> *If you make my word your home...*
> *you will learn the truth*
> *and the truth shall make you free.*
> (Gospel of John 8: 31–32)

Although psychoanalysis is certainly not without pain, as a means toward mental freedom and growth, it is a solemn pleasure indeed.

O and the unity of the soul

These ideas are in the territory of ontology – the metaphysical study of being – which as I have suggested, also includes what from another perspective can be seen as an experience of *nonbeing*. It sounds paradoxical, but as the presence of mind in a real state of being incorporates the half-asleep, nonbeing of O, what Valéry called, the "lack and the blank," it may seem at first glance to be a dissociated state of nonbeing, when it is really a transcendence of one's *known* ego/self. That waking-dream state may evoke a sense of nonbeing that Bion (1970) likened to a regression of the ego, and a feeling of ego-death, but whether for analysts, poets or artists, as well as scientists and mystics, it is hopefully accompanied by a sufficiently knowing self that is able to tolerate those more primitive states. It then becomes a source of mental freedom.

Keats' (1818a) idea of "Negative Capability" is also clearly a part of this experience of the "lack and the blank." In this letter to a friend, Keats clearly describes this as succumbing to an experience of absence or nonbeing, underlying which is a transcendence of the self that is also like a temporary death of the familiar self.

> A Poet is the most unpoetical of any thing in existence; because he has no Identity—he is continually... filling some other Body—the Sun, the Moon, the Sea and Men and Women who are creatures of impulse are poetical and have about them an unchangeable attribute—the poet has none; no identity... no self...
>
> (Keats, 1818b, pp. 337–338)

Very much like Pessoa's idea of becoming, "the thing I feel kinship with," but it is also the analyst's experience of O that facilitates the capacity to transcend the self in the service of at-one-ment with the patient's mind. It differs from pathological states of dissociation or nothingness, for hopefully the analyst has a self to which he or she can return. One cannot, in other words, transcend one's self if one does not yet have a self. Other artists are aware that the waking dream state, like Keats' idea of Negative Capability, is the source and the basis of their work.

> I feel assured I shall write from the mere yearning and fondness I have for the Beautiful even if my night's labors should be burned every morning and no eye ever shine upon them. But even now I am perhaps not speaking from myself; but from some character in whose soul I now live.
>
> (Keats, 1818b, p. 338)

In a sense one *is not oneself* (or at least not one's known ego) in this state of mind, and yet it could equally be said that one is never *more* oneself than when one is in this state. It is the love of higher truth that makes this possible, and rewards one for the discomforts of this temporary disjunction from one's everyday self or mind. For the artist this is everything, as Keats says in his famous last lines from "Ode on a Grecian Urn."

Beauty is truth; truth beauty,
That is all ye know on earth
And all ye need to know.
          (Keats, 1819, p. 253)

This last poem by Pessoa reminded me of Bion's idea of the need to embrace one's ignorance, for Pessoa here writes about one day seeing what he alludes to as the "Great Mystery the false poets speak of."

I saw...
That there are hills, valleys and plains,
That there are trees, flowers and grass,
That there are rivers and stone,
But that there is no whole to which all this belongs,
that a true and real ensemble
Is a disease of our own ideas.
Nature is parts without a whole.
This is perhaps the mystery they speak of.
This is what, without thinking or pausing,
I realized must be the truth
That everyone tries to find but doesn't find
And that I alone found, because I didn't try to find it.
          (Pessoa, 1914, p. 65)

The infinite whole is simply too much for our finite minds to order and comprehend. Despite this inability to fully understand or know the Universe, we can admire it, and even become one with parts of it that impress themselves upon us, and by so doing appreciate the awesome powers before us. We might even happen into an experience of it by accident that convinces us of its majesty, and our own appreciation of it. I am not sure that this is what Pessoa is saying here, or whether wholeness is indeed "a disease of our own ideas." But perhaps the disease is our expectation that we are capable of this grand perspective, rather than respecting the vast depth of our ignorance before such a lofty creation. Perhaps the disease is the belief that we will ever understand it fully, or understand ourselves fully, but that should not deter us from taking a step in that direction, as we work toward our small but powerful glimpses into truth and beauty.

References

Bion, W. R. (1962). *Learning From Experience*. New York: Basic Books

Bion, W. R. (1965). Transformations. In *Seven Servants* (pp 1–183). New York: Jason Aronson, 1977.

Bion, W. R. (1970). *Attention and Interpretation*. London: Karnac.

Bion, W. R. (1979). The dawn of oblivion. In *Memoir of the Future, Book 3* (pp. 427–578). London: Karnac, 1991.

Bion, W. R. (1992). *Cogitations*. London: Karnac.

Grotstein, J. S. (2009). *...But at the Same Time and on Another Level...*" Volume 1. London: Karnac.

Jones, E. (1957). *The Life and Work of Sigmund Freud, Volume 3: The Last Phase*. New York: Basic Books.

Keats, J. (1818a). Letter to George and Tom Keats, 22 December 1818. In P. De Man (Ed.). *The Selected Poetry of Keats* (pp. 328–329). New York, Ontario: Signet Classic New American Library, 1966.

Keats, J. (1818b). Letter to Richard Woodhouse, 27 October 1818. In P. De Man (Ed.). *The Selected Poetry of Keats* (pp. 337–338). New York, Ontario: Signet Classic New American Library, 1966.

Keats, J. (1819). Ode on a Grecian Urn. In P. De Man (Ed.). *The Selected Poetry of Keats* (pp. 252–253). New York, Ontario: Signet Classic New American Library, 1966.

Netburn, D. (2017). A record leap in quantum physics. *Los Angeles Times*, June 17, 2017 (p. 2).

Pessoa, F. (1914). The Keeper of Sheep. In R. Zenith (Ed.) (Trans.). *Fernando Pessoa & Co.* (p. 65). New York: Grove Press, 1998.

Pessoa, F. (1931). In A. Mac Adam (Trans.). *The Book of Disquiet by Fernando Pessoa*. Boston, MA: Exact Change, 1998.

Pessoa, F. (1998). Introduction: The Drama and Dream of Fernando Pessoa. In R. Zenith (Ed.) (Trans.). *Fernando Pessoa & Co.* (p. 57). New York: Grove Press.

Reiner, A. (2008a). *Presents of Mind*. Lancaster, CA: Red Dance Floor Press.

Reiner, A. (2008b). Ode to O. In *Presents of Mind*. Lancaster, CA: Red Dancefloor Press.

Reiner, A. (2017). Ferenczi's 'astra' and Bion's 'O': A clinical perspective. In A. Reiner (Ed.). *Of Things Invisible to Mortal Sight: Celebrating the Work of James S. Grotstein* (pp. 131–148). London: Karnac.

Reiner, A. (2022). *Something to Do With O (But Who Knows)*. Unpublished.

Talbot, M. (1988). *Beyond the Quantum*. New York, Toronto London: Bantam Book/ Macmillan Publishing Co.

Valéry, P. (1950). *Selected Writings of Paul Valéry*. New York: New Directions Publishing Co.

Valéry, P. (1958). *Paul Valéry: The Art of Poetry*. Princeton, NJ: Princeton University Press, Bollingen Series XLV, 7.

Winnicott, C. (1974). Fear of breakdown, D. W. Winnicott. *International Journal of Psychoanalysis*, 1: 102.

Zenith, R. (Trans., Ed.) (1998). *Fernando Pessoa & Co*. New York: Grove Press.

Chapter 5

Spiritual mysticism in the visual arts

Love and truth

In this chapter, we will look at visual artists whose works are at comparable depths as the poetic works we have discussed, works of a more profound nature than those whose aim is purely entertaining or decorative. This is not to imply that they cannot be deeply meaningful and entertaining, and perhaps at best they are both. One of the best examples of this is the work of Henri Matisse. Having grown up in a textile city in Northern France, his innovations in painting, sculpture, and his later medium of paper cut-outs, bore the influence of his lasting interest in the beauty of textiles. While decorative arts like textiles are traditionally meant to adorn, and purely decorative paintings may often be designed to "match the couch," they are much less likely to aim at imparting any serious messages. Matisse wrote about his desire for "an art of balance, of purity and serenity, devoid of troubling or depressing subject matter...a soothing, calming influence on the mind," and yet his works were far from mere adornments, for the purity and serenity to which he aspired were best achieved through his deeper aim of "reducing things to their 'essentials'" (Flam, 1978, p. 21). "There is an inherent truth," he said, "which must be disengaged from the outward appearance of the object to be represented. This is the only truth that matters" (Read, 1974, p. 44). His aim was, "to eliminate what is not essential and what is therefore detrimental to the hypnotic power of the image" (Gilot, 1990, p. 77). In Bion's terms, that essential truth is 'O,' and in both disciplines it is reached through contact with similar kinds of waking dream states, a hypnotic semi-trance that enables the artist, or the analyst, to access and express the essential truth of the physical object. By observing it through one's own emotional experience, it can reveal something new, particular to that artist, in a way that can surprise and awaken something new in the viewer.

While Matisse's later paintings and paper cut-outs are colorful, fanciful and pleasing to the eye, their foundation of underlying solemnity and nutritive value is a function of the artist's inherent sense of artistic truth. He had a rare capacity to capture the essence of whatever he was painting, which transformed it into new shapes of his own creation. It is really a perceptual capacity, an ability to see with his own eyes, and with a child's wonder. It is what Pessoa (1914b) described (in

DOI: 10.4324/9781003470953-6

Chapter 4), as an ability "…to see without thinking… to see when seeing and not think when seeing" (p. 57). By seeing with his own eyes, Matisse transcended the object depicted, creating a new form based on his own intuitive and emotional reality, which represented or symbolized the object, without being enslaved to its actual form.

This process also underlies Bion's (1962) idea of the need for the analyst to intuit the "selected fact," the cogent perspective in a session, which is achieved through a similar focus and discipline that allows access to one's own unique emotional reality, in the waking dream state of O that can distill the session to its essence, and into a thinkable image. It is in line with the idea of O as a reflection of absolute truth, and the Godhead. Along these same lines Matisse wrote, "I believe in God when I work" (Gilot, 1990, p. 193). Like Bion, Matisse differentiated this from a belief in a religious God, as it is the individual's act of artistic inspiration itself, that is the religious experience.

Matisse's ability to simplify and distill an image that could transcend its physical reality, while at the same time revealing something essential about it is a singular gift. It reflects the same capacity for a unified vision that Valéry described in poetry, which is a necessary part of the psychoanalytic perspective of O to transcend one's ego-driven, logical mind. Although Matisse and Picasso were very different kinds of artists and personalities, who had a long, well-documented artistic dialogue, and rivalry, Picasso's profound admiration for Matisse was evident in his statement, "All things considered, there is only Matisse" (Gilot, 1990, p. 316).

Paintings of being, paintings of O

In examining similar issues of spiritual connection to those we have seen in poets' works, we will look at the works of postmodern and contemporary visual artists, Mark Rothko, Jackson Pollack and Jean Arp. Starting chronologically, I will start with Arp, and with Dadaism, that arose in the period of agitation following World War I. We will then look at the movement in post–World War II artists who were interested in painting the spiritual or sublime, but in ways very different from the overt depictions of religious subject matter that had characterized spiritual and religious yearnings in ancient and Renaissance art. The works of these new painters, often Abstract Expressionists like Robert Motherwell, Pollack, Rothko and others, seemed to depict spiritual experience through the *form* of their paintings, rather than primarily just the *content*. These were direct expressions of pure being, and of being in the moment, and this, like O, required a sense of oneness with, and immersion in, the moment of creation.

Dada, Arp and Bion's O

Jean Arp was a visionary French/German painter, sculptor and poet, who was a leader of the European avant-garde at the beginning of the 20th century. His legacy is closely tied to the Dada movement, of which he was an early member.

Arp viewed Dadaism as a revolutionary art form, a protest against the traditional logic and morality of bourgeois thinking, which was also seen to reflect an evolution of the human mind. The aim of the Dadaist poets and artists was to coax a dream-like mental state into consciousness.

> It was in dreams that I learned how to write, and it was only much later that I laboriously learned how to read.
>
> (Arp, 1972, p. xv)

The primacy of dreams is obviously echoed in Bion's emphasis on the importance of the waking-dream state of O in analytic work, and with his idea of dreams as a form of unconscious thinking that was the foundation for more developed capacities to think. For Bion, dreaming was the basis of the development of our capacity to think, making dreams central to all mental development. In this way, Arp's idea about Dada as an evolution of the human mind, and Dada's satirical, playful, sometimes nonsensical tone, also elevated the dream state to a primary position. In part it was a reaction to the horrors of a war that revealed an essential error in the mind and mores of the culture. Dada is an art of "Chance," a 20th century phenomenon which aims to give up control and choice, for a non-deliberative, serendipitous accident. To this end, Arp did a well-known picture in 1916 called, "Collage Arranged According to the Laws of Chance" (Lipsey, 1988, pp. 119–120). In its creation, he dropped random sizes of colored paper squares onto a board or paper, which he subsequently glued in place. This apparent randomness represented "the order of nature" or "an inexplicable reason" (Lipsey, 1988, p. 119.). We can also view it as a reliance on unseen forces of an untapped, unconscious order, that Dadaists saw as a power to be uncovered and utilized. This is on the same model as the "wisdom" of the unconscious, and Freud's technique of listening to a patient's free associations which, if properly read, can reveal messages from the deep. It may be no accidental synchronicity that Arp's early works roughly coincided with Freud's early psychoanalytic theories of dreams and the unconscious.

Dada's attempts to supplant logic through the *seeming* illogic of accidental, gestural, unconscious movement, is characterized by humor, spontaneity, irrationality and anarchism, a kind of playful, child-like quality that belies the wisdom of the vast, although *unknown logic* of the unconscious it reflects. This was not anarchy for the sake of anarchy, but an attempt to integrate the unknown, unknowable, and so only *seemingly* anarchic vastness of unconscious mental life into the comparatively shrunken lives of our rational egos. The unconscious, which includes imagination, creativity, potential genius and potential madness, had to be given center stage, released from the rigid prison of logic that promises us protection from those dangerous, untamed mental waters, but in the process oppresses the creative forces of life. Like the accidental works of artists, the automatic writing of Dada poets were efforts to give voice to the enormous raw power of mental energy within. In a way these are efforts to introduce that transcendent self, spirit or soul to our much more limited everyday selves. The difference in scope of these very different aspects of our minds is expressed by Heraclitus, the sixth century Greek philosopher.

> You could not discover the limits of the soul, even if you traveled by every path in order to do so; such is the depth of its meaning.
>
> Heraclitus (in Lipsey, op. cit., p. 9)

Arp's poetry and art were part of that quest for the daunting power of that spontaneous inner truth to replace, or perhaps ultimately to augment, the measured formality of classical art, and of the logical mind.

The word "Dada" derived from a combination of "Da Da" – the Roumanian word for "yes" – and the French word for a child's rocking horse. It reflected the essential optimism, and playful joy and freedom of the child. In "The Who's" rock opera, *Tommy*, the main character is a "deaf, dumb and blind kid" who is masterful at playing pinball, not unlike the Dada artist who makes himself deaf, dumb and blind, the better to rely on instinct. It is also essentially like Freud's suggestion that the analyst has to "artificially blind" himself, in order to focus on that which cannot literally be seen, heard, or touched. This is another way in which the concerns of the Dada movement overlapped with the beginning of psychoanalysis, both in their emphasis on the importance of the mental life of the child, as well as the vast hidden power of the unconscious. It is also very much in line with Bion's description of the experience of the unknown and unknowable O, where the analyst must be "... in a peculiar state of mind [where] the margin between being consciously awake... and being asleep, is extremely small" (Bion, 1978, p. 41). This peculiar waking dream state is a kind of trance state that allows access to the wisdom carried in our dreams. The random, non-deliberative nature of Dada art is what Bion (1977) called the need for the analyst to entertain and attend to "stray thoughts," "wild thoughts" and "thoughts without a thinker" (p. 27), and to exercise "speculative imagination" (Bion, 1977, p. 47). However, Bion's view also requires the analyst to satisfy scientific truth, which includes the ability to recognize and present evidence for whatever is being intuited or imagined.

> On the way to being an analyst, you have to reserve the right to indulge your speculations, your speculative imagination... to give your imagination an airing, to give it a chance to develop into something that might be scientific.
>
> (Bion, 1977, p. 47)

Imagination is thus a first step which may provide necessary information, which can then be tested by the additional evidence within the material in a session. Bion makes it clear that we cannot simply imagine anything we want, without further evidence. As he put it, one cannot, "disconnect your mind from your jaw" and just say whatever one likes. And yet these sometimes wild conjectures and speculations provide freedom to the mind that can facilitate the emergence of something new. There are differences between these states of mental freedom in psychoanalysis and the arts, for Arp's poetry, and the liberation from logic that is Dada, does not bear that same kind of responsibility to fortify its imaginative fancies with *scientific* truth. However the artist is beholden to a capacity for *aesthetic* truth. The sense of freedom derived from releasing the mind from the stultification of overly rational forces is supported and strengthened by the aesthetic or artistic truth of the artist, not unlike the analyst's need for evidence for what one intuits.

Stop Making Sense

Stop Making Sense is the title of a 1984 documentary about the rock band, "The Talking Heads," and David Byrne's brilliantly wild and quirky lyrics make him a fitting heir to Dada. But he too is clearly responsible to his own aesthetic truth, which provides its own unconscious "logic" beneath the apparent nonsense of some of the lyrics. "Stop making sense" is also a fair suggestion for how to free one's mind for contact with O, or for understanding these lines by Arp.

> *I like to reckon slowly slowly*
> *but incorrectly...*
> *I like miscalculations*
> *for they offer*
> *more accurate results.*
> *Likewise I like to*
> *reckon painstakingly*
> *without obtaining any result.*
> (Arp, 1972, p. xviii)

Finding the result cannot be the active aim, whether in art, science or psychoanalysis. The aim is toward the mental freedom that might lead to something new, some serendipitous revelation. Like Keats' Negative Capability, results cannot be actively sought, and Arp's preference, "To reckon slowly but incorrectly," seems also to reflect this idea that the aim isn't to be correct by any already existing standard, but to open one's dreaming mind to the possibility of a new standard of truth for that moment. It is an endeavor that is beyond the right or wrong of what is already known, for either may bear fruit, and either may get one closer to a truth one does not know, and can only dream of.

Mark Rothko

Art historian, Roger Lipsey (1988), wrote, "The burden of art, at its best, is to still words by bringing other kinds of perception to the center of awareness" (p. 308). In my experience, Rothko was masterful at doing exactly that. In the distinctive style of his creative maturity in the 1950s and 1960s, Rothko managed to "still words" and transport the viewer, not just to a different place, but to what felt like a universal place beyond everyday space and time. In his seemingly simple abstract designs, often two or three stacked rectangles of different sizes and various, but increasingly dark colors, one could feel an almost eerie silence, and get a peculiar sense of movement in the painterly brush strokes that belie the simplicity of the compositions.

Dore Ashton, an art critic and Rothko's friend, described a visit to his studio, where she saw Rothko's large new paintings in a dimly lit space, "as though I had walked into a theater, or an ancient library... Rothko watched my reaction as I examined the arrangement of large canvases and said, 'I have made a place... They are not pictures'" (Lipsey, 1988, p. 308). This was precisely my impression of them too, for there was a sense of being drawn into this "place" he had created, a kind of magical place. In fact this feeling inspired in me the story of a children's book that I had been asked to write and illustrate about modern and contemporary art. Standing in front of Rothko's painting the story came to me. I suddenly had my book, for I envisioned two small children standing in front of one of these Rothko paintings with a dark rectangular field at the top, like a dark undulating night sky, and I watched as they were transported into the artist's magical "place." I called the book, *A Visit to the Art Galaxy*, and as these children made their way through the museum, they were transported into the galaxies of their own imaginations, through each of the subsequent works they encountered, from Matisse and Picasso to Franz Kline and the skinny shadows of people in a Giacometti sculpture, and finally to conceptual artists like Chris Burden (Reiner, 1990).

Even before he found his distinctive style, Rothko often spoke of transcendent or spiritual themes in his art. Again, this visual rendering of a spiritual place was very different from Medieval or Renaissance paintings whose subject matter was religious, but which may or may not have imparted the intense sense of awe evoked by Rothko's paintings. The "place" he had created was both an inner space of pure mind or spirit, and a sense of a vast outer universe as well. The narratives of the myths depicted in earlier religious paintings whose stories we already knew, sometimes made it more difficult to, as Lipsey said, "still the words," but Rothko's paintings had an odd power to still the words, but to stop time too with their uncanny ability to depict a timeless inner or outer world.

In this way, Rothko's later paintings seem to me to be depictions of O. They are unique abstract glimpses into a mental universe beyond the known self, that somehow manage to capture the essence of a vast physical universe as well. It does not surprise me that Rothko once said of these later paintings, "I wanted to paint both the finite and the infinite" (Ashton, 1996, p. 179). What is mysterious in the paintings is how so much life and vitality inheres in the often very dark and simply composed paintings. All three color fields seem to be teeming with energy, as they overlap and infiltrate each other's boundaries. They also seem to depict the un-depictable emptiness of an infinite mind that facilitates one's vision into this transcendent realm, giving the viewer the cosmic experience of awe described by Einstein (above, Chapter 3).

Not everyone appreciated these quiet, contemplative paintings, which were described by some critics as baffling, empty or mysterious. It is not so different from the kinds of responses Bion's concept of O received, which depicted an unknowable universe of a similar breadth and depth. Interestingly, these paintings were made during the 1960s, at approximately the time that Bion first wrote about O in 1965. These works of Rothko's culminated in a commission he received to do a series of enormous paintings for what was to become the Rothko Chapel in Houston (Ashton, 1996, pp. 183–184). When I visited the Chapel and walked into the serene octagonal space, I saw fourteen huge dark paintings, 11 to 15 feet high, in what looked like monochromatic black. I was perplexed at first, but when I got closer to each painting I could see vague differentiations of what used to be more distinct fields of color, although almost indistinct from each other. Upon even closer inspection, the paint seemed to undulate and radiate with light, making them seem even more like a window into the cosmos. Their mythic quality, and incandescent undulations imparted a religious feeling, for me a secular spiritual- ity like Bion's O, but which gave an almost psychedelic sense to the experience. It was inexplicable how so much life and movement could be emitted from such seemingly still, dark paintings. Some people commented on these fluctuations of light and the transcendent quality, while others found it too austere. In my view, Rothko managed to represent his communion with an invisible sense of the divine that infused these paintings. Just as Milton (1667) attempted to give verbal form to celestial light, when finding himself in "…the rising world of waters dark and deep/ Won from the void and formless infinite" (p. 63), Rothko seemed to have given shape to the same shapeless, formless infinite.

If the artist's mind is in that universal space, in the state of mind of O, it can somehow make it onto the canvas to be seen, for any viewer who has "eyes to see" that metaphysical vision beyond our physical organs of perception. I thought that Rothko's bond with that transcendent realm of O was indicated by this very telling comment, "I don't express myself in my painting, I express my not self" (Lipsey, 1988, p. 316). As discussed in the previous chapter, this "not self," engaged in the waking-dream of O, is a transcendent mind or self that is beyond the known and physical self, and so is a sort of not self.

Access to this more expansive self may feel more like oneself than one's familiar known self, but it may also feel like nonexistence. And so we also see something here of the dangers Bion warned about, the ego regression and loss of a sense of self if one becomes submerged in the vast, formless mental universe without suf- ficient preparation. I don't know if this was so for Rothko, but he did experience a severe depression in these years, which ended with his suicide in 1970 (Lipsey, 1988, pp. 318–319). Several other factors contributed to this tragic end, including his having been diagnosed with an aortal aneurysm, and suffering a tremendous loss when his studio burned down, along with many of his beloved paintings. Still, the dangers that Bion warned about were real, for having contact with an unknown and unknowable dream world could lead to a sense of having lost oneself if one's primitive feelings had not been resolved.

The Rothko Chapel opened in Houston in 1971, a year after Mark Rothko's death.

Jackson Pollack

The idea of a transcendent self was also vividly depicted in Jackson Pollack's "drip" paintings. Even his method of painting, standing over his huge canvases on the floor, gave him the sense of being inside the painting. When Hans Hoffman, the famous art teacher, suggested that he do some paintings "after Nature," Pollack protested, "I *am* Nature" (Lipsey, 1988, p. 305). Indeed, Pollack's artistic style, his visual "voice" or "character" as it were, were direct expressions of his deepest nature, of O. Bion (1970) said of O, "It can be 'become' but it cannot be 'known'" (p. 26), and so the analyst must "*be* it" (p. 27). While many people, past and present, have criticized Pollack's splatter technique as being so primitive that anyone could do it, even a child, or that they are chaotic and fragmented, on closer inspection they represent a surprisingly integrated world. What is remarkable about the work is an uncanny, underlying order and integrity. As we know about dreams, their apparent chaos also reveals a surprisingly cogent underlying order and meaning, and Pollack's paintings are another masterful example of O, the visual creation of the underlying order in that mystical, waking-dream state. These often huge gestural paintings do seem random, drips and splotches that spill from his brush, but they reveal the presence of an unexpected unifying capacity that creates that sense of oneness in which each "splotch" seems to have its perfect place in an integrated whole. It is a bit like an organized city but rather than being planned and carefully erected, it is just poured out fully formed, just as dreams come without any apparent effort from us. Pollack does seem to have created these works in a waking-dream state, an unconscious creation of an abstract universe that seems too complex to have been created by a mere, and seemingly careless, human. And yet that is the point about O, it is on some outer reach of our human capacities, which is why artists and scientists are driven to make contact with it, to be a part of its order, wisdom and magic. The following is a description by Betty Parsons, a painter who was also Pollack's first art dealer.

> How hard Jackson could work, and with such grace!... He was like a dancer. He had the canvas on the floor with cans of paint around the edges that had sticks in them which he'd seize and—swish and swish again. There was such rhythm in his movement... [His compositions]... were so complex, yet he never went overboard—always in perfect balance... When Jackson would get lost, I think the unconscious took over and that's marvelous.
>
> (Lipsey, 1988, p. 303)

I think the criticism that Pollack was doing something a child could do was not without merit, but to see this as a criticism is missing the point. As described earlier, the capacity for at-one-ment with O that Bion saw as a psychoanalytic imperative, does indeed depend on the capacity for contact with the infant mind, with the openness and awesome breadth of the oceanic feeling. In any creative endeavor, contact with O requires contact with that very primitive state of mind of a child. And yet, as discussed in Chapter 3, the analyst or poet, artist, mystic, genius or scientist who seeks access to that infinite infant mind, must *also* be armed with the capacity for more evolved abilities to contain and think about one's primal experiences. Parson's description of Pollack's graceful dance while painting, speaks to his capacity to contain that chaotic primitive mind in his work. Bion's idea about the constant oscillations in adult life between the primitive paranoid schizoid and depressive anxieties (Ps]D), reflect this need for integration between these two opposing levels of mental functioning. The analyst, according to Bion, needs to experience both these levels in creating a cogent interpretation.

While this kind of integration is rare, it does not necessarily mean that one can tolerate such feelings outside the boundaries of their creative work, and it is no secret that Pollack was a troubled, often haunted, man. One's capacity to use those primitive feelings in creative work is a gift, but does not insure that this enormous amount of mental and emotional energy can be held outside the work.

While Rothko and Pollack, and other abstract painters in that generation of artists in the 1950s and 1960s, were interested in spirituality in their work, Pollack distinguishes it from traditional forms of religion, as Bion does in his concept of O.

> Churches are okay if you got to belong to something to feel safe, but artists don't need that… they're part of the universal energy in their creating. Look—existence **is.** We're part of all like everything else, we're on our own, goddamit!
>
> (Lipsey, 1988, p. 306).

Not only, as Pollack says, do artists not need the safety that the Church provides, in fact they need to cultivate a tolerance for the *un*safety of the unknown, for the existential fear of being on one's own. Paradoxically, it is that capacity to relinquish reliance on that primitive God that enables a real sense of safety when one discovers that one can endure the unknown, and find that a higher, more knowing self has taken over. While some artists or writers feel that someone or something external to them has taken over, a Muse or God, in secular terms it is an internal connection to one's own divine self, one's godhood, which has its roots in the dream-like mind of one's infant self, who has no choice but to be connected to the energy of all that is.

Likewise for the analyst, only by tolerating the fear of letting go of all one knows, can one make contact with that infant mind, and with O. Bion (1970) describes this as an act of faith, but for him "faith" is "a scientific state of mind" (p. 32). He wrote, "The 'act of faith' (F) depends on disciplined denial of memory and desire" (p. 41). And so for Bion, one's faith is not for an omnipotent, external God, but faith in the existence of Truth, if one can work toward contact with one's internal godhood. It is the faith that if we can tolerate not knowing, we make mental space for the higher Truth to emerge, for at least in that moment we have made ourselves part of the universal energy.

Part of the fear of the blank page, or the blank canvas, is the fear of being judged, and like so many innovative artists or thinkers, Pollack certainly was judged for work that others did not understand. It can derail some artists from their work, but it can also strengthen them, as one is forced then to learn to trust that transcendent voice before all others, even if no one else understands. New Truths are not always popular, and to get beyond the petty judgments of others, or oneself, that inhibit creativity, can be lonely and frightening.

Like Nietzsche's (1886) idea of an elevated state of mind, "beyond good and evil," which we will look at in the next chapter, Bion (1965) points out that O is always beyond judgment. O "is not good or evil," he states, "it cannot be known, loved, or hated" (p. 139). O, in other words, or absolute Truth, just is. This will not keep others from judging the work of those, like Pollack, who create something new in that waking dream state of O. As we saw, his paintings were deemed "bad" because they did not fit into previous ideas of what art should look like. New ideas and innovations in art often receive censure as people are forced to throw out their old standards in order to understand something new, but it is not so different for the analyst. Our patients do not always like our interpretations, and the resistance to them can be fierce. But if they are true, we will have to say them anyway. It is then up to the analytic couple to determine whether or not the interpretation is in fact true, and if so, what objection the patient has to Truth. Patients have greater or lesser degrees of openness to their own psychological truths, which may be received with some fear and resistance. Each developmental step reveals an illusion in which we have believed, but whether in art or psychoanalysis, if we can learn to strengthen our capacity for Truth, despite our fear, it may be accompanied by a sense of awe and beauty that are inherent in growth.

References

Arp, J. (1972). *Arp on Arp*. New York: Penguin/Random House.

Ashton, D. (1996). *About Rothko*. New York: Da Capo Press.

Bion, W. R. (1962). *Learning from Experience,* New York: Basic Books.

Bion, W. R. (1965). Transformations. In *Seven Servants* (pp. 1–183). New York: Jason Aronson, 1977.

Bion, W. R. (1970). *Attention and Interpretation*. London: Karnac.

Bion, W. R. (1977). In F. Bion (Ed.). *Taming Wild Thoughts* (pp. 27–38). London: Karnac Books, 1997.

Bion, W. R. (1978). *Four Discussion with W. R. Bion*. Perthshire: Cluny Press.

Flam, J. D. (1978). *Matisse on Art*. New York: E. P. Dutton.

Gilot, F. (1990). *Matisse and Picasso: A Friendship in Art*. New York: Doubleday Dell Publishing Group.

Lipsey, R. (1988). *The Spiritual in Twentieth Century Art*. Mineola, NY: Dover Publications.

Milton, J. (1667). Paradise Lost, Book III. In *Paradise Lost and Paradise Regained* (pp. 62–81). New York: Airmont Publishing Company, 1968.

Nietzsche, F. (1886). *Beyond ood and Evil*. In R. J. Hollingdale (Trans.). London, New York: Penguin Books, 1973.

Pessoa, F. (1914b). The Keeper of Sheep. In R. Zenith (Ed.) (Trans.). *Fernando Pessoa & Co.* (pp. 45–65). New York, Grove Press, 1998.

Read, H. (1974). *A Concise History of Modern Painting*. London: Thames & Hudson.

Reiner, A. (1990). *A Visit to the Art Galaxy*. New York: Green Tiger Press/Simon & Shuster.

Reiner, A. (2008). Ode to O. In *Presents of Mind*. Lancaster, CA: Red Dancefloor Press.

Chapter 6

The ancient wisdom is still new

Aspiring after true being in Plato, Nietzsche and Bion

Phaedo, in Plato's *Republic*, is an account of the discussion that took place on the day that the imprisoned Socrates was to die, but even in the face of death, his unwavering commitment was to truth (Plato, 1942). Refusing to be silenced, he continued teaching his friends gathered around him, about the knowledge of true being, for which he was willing to give his life. It seems worth asking why the ancient wisdom about what it means to be human, according to great philosophical, artistic and religious minds, still seems like news to us. I will examine here why aspects of this higher knowledge are sometimes still alien to psychoanalysts who are engaged in a similar pursuit for knowledge of consciousness, morality, mortality and being. It is worth noting, however, that these ideas were never widely accepted, and so despite his devotion to truth, Socrates was put to death for crimes vaguely described as corrupting the youth, and impiety against state-approved gods. Even the pursuit of religious truths in the Bible, widely disseminated throughout the world quickly led to *distortions* of those truths almost from the beginning. As mentioned above in Chapter 3, the distinction between the beliefs put forth in the early Christian Gospels and the mystical beliefs of the Gnostic Gospels, reflect the legacy of that ancient wisdom that was already effectively corrupted, for the Gnostics saw Jesus as a teacher of divine wisdom that each individual must learn, as opposed to the belief in Jesus as a reified God whose wisdom and power is imparted through magical or ritualised means. In the ritual of the holy Eucharist, the wine and wafers, meant to symbolize the blood and the body of Christ, is more like a concretised symbol experienced as equivalent to the thing itself, rather than a mental representation of an abstract thought (Segal, 1981). It is the difference between a physically, or metaphysically, based reality. This ritualistic ingestion of the blood and body of Christ, in other words, comes to differ essentially from the metaphysical work of a mind involved in the development of one's own search for a higher self, for the consciousness and conscience that is the message of the Gnostics.

DOI: 10.4324/9781003470953-7

Genesis of morality and consciousness

The confusion between these two very different endeavors suggests that one of the reasons Bion's idea of the mental apprehension of the mystical O is still so controversial is that knowledge of that infinite and absolute truth is simply so difficult for our finite minds to apprehend. It is perhaps on these grounds that mystical ideas appear to have been forbidden from the beginning. In *Genesis,* Adam and Eve are tempted by the serpent to eat the forbidden fruit of the Tree of Knowledge of Good and Evil. It is purported to mean that by eating the fruit, the human inclination for evil is born, where before that Man was pure and good. The idea of this birth of an appetite for evil came to include the temptations of the flesh, including sex. This mythological/literary construct has been interpreted in many ways that do not necessarily include an awareness of divine knowledge which, the myth goes, is forbidden by God. It is widely interpreted to mean that what was forbidden was *carnal* knowledge, despite the fact that the "knowledge of good and evil" put it squarely in the metaphysical realm of the mind rather than the physical realm of the body. The implication is that only God is good, although according to Bion the Godhead, or O, is neither good nor bad, it is simply the truth, deeper truths that exist whether or not we understand them. Is a child evil, for instance, if he hates his mother, or his father, and wishes them dead? It would seem so, as there is even a commandment against that – "Thou shalt honor they mother and father." But what if that mother or father has in some way neglected or abused the child? What if, as Jesus seems to indicate, a parent is not in line with "God," with the higher, absolute Truth, and so conflicts with the child's inherent sense of what is right?

> If anyone declares himself for me in the presence of men, I will declare myself for him in the presence of my Father in heaven. But the one who disowns me in the presence of men, I will disown in the presence of my Father in heaven.
>
> (Matthew, 10: 32–33)

This addresses the cost of one's awareness, or lack of awareness, of higher truth. In Chapter 4, I quoted Christ's statement that he "[has] not come to bring peace to the world, but a sword ... I have come to set a man against his father, a daughter against her mother" (Jerusalem Bible, Matthew 10: 34–36). We saw there that Arjuna's plight was the same as that which Jesus speaks of here, that the consequences of a breach of these higher truths within family relations also leads to a personal war in which, "one's enemies... [are] those of his own household." (ibid.)

Judgments of good or evil, in other words, are variable depending upon the circumstances of any given situation. One's intentions are not necessarily easy to know, but one's capacity to understand the whole picture will determine whether or not one will be able to apprehend the truth. But this is a revolutionary idea, and it is for difficult ideas like this that Christ is seen as revolutionary. Almost two centuries later, Nietzsche (1886) addressed a very similar issue, and it was still revolutionary, for he said that an action can only be determined to be good or bad

based on the *intentions behind the act*, not by the act itself. The reason it is so difficult is that there cannot then be a rigid set of rules about good and evil. This makes
morality a far more complex matter than blindly learning to follow an established
list of commandments, for without knowing one's own intentions, or the intentions
of the other, one cannot judge an action. Religions and social mores may reflect
only the simplest common denominator that may apply to the greatest number of
instances, but a higher morality cannot evolve from that level of thinking. Only
the deeper knowledge of the mystic can point us in the direction of this infinitely
more complex task of true morality. This also underlies Freud's notion of a need to
know one's unconscious intentions in order to understand the nature and meaning
of one's actions. And so the mystic may be religious, or secular like Nietzsche and
Freud, and the secular mysticism of Bion's O.

The controversy surrounding the concept of O is difficult to resolve, or even to
address, for to know something of this metaphysical reality, one must transcend the
dominant, although limited, function of rational thinking, in order to intuit those
often unconscious intentions behind an action. This task for the analyst is not to
judge but to find the unconscious truth. It is also the idea behind Rumi's poem.

> Out beyond ideas of wrongdoing and rightdoing
> there is a field. I will meet you there.
>
> (Rumi, 2003, p. 123)

Of course, this is not a place that is easy to find, nor is it really a place at all, but
a mental space, of being, rather than judging. If the analyst is judging, either the
patient or oneself, he or she will be unable to access that intuitive mind that allows
contact with O, and with the patient.

As mentioned in Chapter 3, Grotstein called O "the transcendent position," a
capacity that extends beyond Klein's conception of the mind.

> …[O]ne who has become O, has traversed beyond the depressive position and
> attained the "transcendent position… He has now become an "ubermensch,"
> "higher man."
>
> (Grotstein, 2007, p. 3)

Grotstein associates this ideal of mental transcendence with Nietzsche's Uber-
mensch, a term variously described by Nietzsche (1886) as "the new philosopher," and "the new psychologist," or "psychologist of the future," which he also
called "the man of tomorrow and the day after tomorrow" (pp. 136–137, sec. 211).
Clearly, this was not something we were yet capable of, it would take more mental development. Nietzsche also called them, "friends of truth" (Nietzsche, 1886,
p. 53), and I would say that Bion is one of those friends of truth, a psychologist of
the future who was nonetheless in our midst, the kind of psychologist for whom
Nietzsche was impatiently waiting. All the terms he used to describe what we as a
species are awaiting, reflect the idea of a *secular* mysticism.

In Nietzsche's (1885) *Thus Spoke Zarathustra,* the prophet, Zarathustra, notes that the so-called "good and just" people did not understand Jesus, because, "… their spirit is imprisoned in their good conscience. The stupidity of the good is unfathomably clever" (p. 229). He continues:

Whatever harm the wicked may do, the harm the good do is the most harmful harm!

While the God of religion may be seen as the epitome of goodness, the Godhead, O, is about truth that exceeds established boundaries of good and evil, and questions the simplicity of this moral dichotomy. Like O, the knowledge of this kind of absolute truth is unreachable by our finite selves. It is Adam and Eve's sinful curiosity about this divine knowledge of good and evil 'that' gets them ejected from God's garden, but what if we simply don't know what these intuitive writers of the Bible were talking about? And what did they themselves understand about the complexities of the good and evil aspects of mankind? Bion concluded that we do not really understand what a human mind is, in part because of all our false assumptions that became Church dogma, or psychoanalytic dogma, false assumptions based on oversimplication and overly rigid duality.

It is easy to see how our own *inability to understand this divine and elusive mind* can come to be misinterpreted as a God who does not *want* us to know about this mysterious level of experience, thus making it forbidden. But are these states of transcendent being forbidden by a higher being, or does God represent the fact that we are just unable to access it, and choose to blame an all-knowing God, rather than ourselves? That God may then represent an internal imago who warns us that we are in over our heads in this divine infinite realm, and so should not even try. From this perspective, the forbidding God may stand for the punishing super-ego God that is trying to "protect" us from the pain of our own mental limitation, our incapacity for higher thoughts. It is essentially a "protection" from our own ignorance, given the elusive work it would take to overcome that ignorance. Something of these questions is expressed in the following poem.

Eve's Big Idea

When we tell the truth
we have glass bodies
and can see all the way through
to our birthdays–
the candles
and the blood.
When we tell the truth
we are whirling
in a child's dizzy nowhere.
Decorating our festive heads
with love sonnets

and Spring bonnets.
Honest is embrace,
where you give me the fruit
I give you
and we lose all sense
of who is who.
See God dance!
See God play!
He didn't say we couldn't eat the fruit–
he just wondered aloud
if we could stand it.
                    (Reiner, 2002, p. 37)

One thing is clear, our familiar, finite, egoistic selves are incapable of contact with this kind of knowledge of absolute truth, the "transcendent position" to which Grotstein alluded, and so Bion postulated a different state of mind – O – that can incorporate an unconscious dream-like self, which is also beyond reach. Bion addressed this mysterious idea about how we come to think unthought thoughts previously beyond our awareness, ideas that might be dreamt, intuited or imagined but cannot yet be entertained as thoughts, the "thoughts without a thinker" whose meanings may be completely unknown to us.

> Thinking is a development forced upon the psyche by the pressure of thoughts and not the other way around.
>
>   (Bion, 1962, p. 111)

This idea differs from the common assumption that we have thoughts because we think or create them with minds we somehow come fully equipped to think with. Bion's (1970) idea suggests that proto-mental, unthinkable "thoughts" exist, and that we need to develop a mind with which to think them, for the pressure of those unknown truths exerts itself on us to think them.

The assumption that ordinary humans are incapable of growth *toward* God's infinite knowledge, or that the chasm between our finite and infinite selves is so abysmal as to be insurmountable, may indeed be currently true, which is why we need mystics and geniuses to help open our minds to further development. Bion's (1970) suggestion that maybe even analysts do not believe in the existence of the mind, raised the question of whether we can continue to develop a mind with the potential to think things we are in fact not yet able to think, and what is involved in the development of that different way of thinking.

Religion and psychoanalysis

I have written at length about the stigma in psychoanalysis against religious thought, which stems in part from Freud's atheism, as well as his concern that religious ideas might tarnish the reputation of psychoanalysis as a science (Reiner, 2009). Freud's view of religion as a neurosis, and an illusion, and of God as the child's idealised view of the father was correct as far as it went, for it accurately describes much of the dogmatic thinking that we see in religious Institutions. It did not, however, account for the metaphysical experiences that had always reflected deeper levels of religious ideas, and it leaves out the possibility of the further development of mental capacities that Bion introduced into psychoanalysis with his concept of O. Freud's beliefs limit the psychoanalytic perspective on religion to its most primitive level, for in overlooking real and valuable aspects of religious experiences of awe that are a natural part of human experience, it unfortunately also removed these aspects of the ancient philosophical and psychological wisdom that is the foundation of religious thought. Through O Bion introduced this into psychoanalytic thought.

As a literary conceit, the God in Genesis is the embodiment of a taboo against the mind-expanding knowledge of our own higher morality. This primitive super-ego God has long dominated people's minds by empowering the fear of and resistance to esoteric knowledge and mental change. We are supposed to love, adore and obey this higher Being of pure goodness, to keep us on the righteous path, but if, like Freud's idea of religion, God is the idealised parent, we remain His adoring children whose deeper understanding of ourselves is split off or repressed. We are thus forbidden to grow up, and to evolve toward a truly moral sense of our own, for stuck in that primitive state, we can only devote ourselves to a God/parent who masks our fear of a task felt to be too difficult to attempt, or even to fathom. Adam's and Eve's "sin" seems to be their curiosity about a divine part of them that, if entertained, would first mean having to do battle with one's own inner forces against a new kind of development of the self.

"God is dead"

Some of these ideas are reflected in Nietzsche's (1882) famous pronouncement, "God is dead," which did not mean only that religion was dead, but that a true religious experience had been *killed* by the simplistic definitions, and distortions, of the Christian Church. According to Nietzsche, and in keeping with Bion's (1970) idea of the reactionary nature of the Establishment, the loyalty to Church dogma had destroyed the infinitely complex idea of divine knowledge, and the understanding of God as a representation of that divine knowledge at the heart of real morality and consciousness. Nietzsche's words below are attributed to "the madman" (presumably himself) who would dare to question the prevailing notion of God.

Do we hear nothing as yet of the noise of the gravediggers who are burying God? Do we smell nothing as yet of the divine decomposition? Gods, too, decompose. God is dead... And we have killed him... What after all are these churches now if they are not the tombs and sepulchers of God?

(Nietzsche, 1882, pp. 181–182/Section 125)

What may seem to the powers-that-be to represent the ravings of a madman, a nihilistic statement *against* religion, was for Nietzsche an attempt to rescue true religious feeling from the hypocrisy and sterility of the Church. It was an attempt to protect the righteousness of true morality from the pious pretensions of Christianity that masqueraded as morality. As he put it,

> [T]he religious person is an exception in every religion.
>
> (Nietzsche, 1882, p. 185/Section 128)

For Nietzsche (1886) the Church Orthodoxy had killed God, and only the death of these already debased notions of God could make room for a higher morality "beyond good and evil," and the evolution toward authentic consciousness.

Nietzsche's revolutionary ideas are consistent with the confusion and disdain still generated by Bion's concept of O. The capacity to experience this evolving level of truth, or even to be aware of it, was still felt to remain in an inaccessible future, and despite Bion's popularity, it seems that his ideas continue to make him a "man of tomorrow." The psychoanalytic revolution that his ideas set in motion are still challenging to our finite minds, for in general, we have not yet attained, or even found a way to work *toward,* the capacity to think in the way that Bion associated with O, which he saw as the necessary psychoanalytic perspective. In Bion's (1970) terms, the inherent wisdom of the mystics and visionaries had been eclipsed by religions that promulgated institutional dogma, destroying the vital underlying truths. His concept of O is an attempt to restore these truths, consistent with the beliefs, not only of secular religious figures, but of scientists and artists as well.

Bion is not exactly saying that every psychoanalyst is or must be a seer or mystic, but he is introducing into analysis the metaphysical aspect of the mind so that we can begin to strive toward the unity of a mental potential with which we are endowed as human beings. Much of the ancient wisdom charted similar courses of evolution toward Nietzsche's vision of the person of the future. Bion did not take this challenge lightly.

> [The] analyst must get hardened to mental breakdowns and become reconciled to the feeling of *continuously* breaking down. That is the price which we have to pay for growth.
>
> (Bion, 1975, p. 206)

Á propos of this daunting challenge, Bion often repeated the story of a Navy Admiral who required a new ship, but was informed by the shipbuilder that it would take 300 years to grow the necessary trees to build the ship. The Admiral replied, "Then we haven't a moment to lose." Likewise, we can either start now in an effort to work toward our own hope for evolution, or be so intimidated by the massive challenge, and by our own fear of change, that we do nothing. Given the serious issues we currently face as human beings – climate change, deadly wars, as well as worldwide political situations in which hate is embraced and truth is unashamedly devalued and denied – it has become even more clear, as that Admiral asserted, that we haven't a moment to lose. While the challenge Bion set before us may barely be imaginable, we cannot afford not to try.

References

Bion, W. R. (1962). A theory of thinking. In *Second Thoughts* (pp. 110–119). New York: Jason Aronson, 1967.

Bion, W. R. (1970). *Attention and Interpretation*. London: Karnac.

Bion, W. R. (1975). *Bion's Brazilian Lectures 2: Rio/Sao Paulo*. Rio de Janeiro: Imago Editora LTDA.

Genesis. (1968). *The New Jerusalem Bible: Readers Edition*. New York: Doubleday & Company, Inc.

Grotstein, J. (2007). *A Beam of Intense Darkness*. London: Karnac.

Milton, J. (1667). *Paradise Lost, Book III*. In *Paradise Lost and Paradise Regained* (pp. 62–81). New York: Airmont Publishing Company, 1968.

Nietzsche, F. (1882). *The Gay Science*. In W. Kaufmann (Trans.). New York: Vantage Books/Random House, 1974.

Nietzsche, F. (1885). *Thus Spoke Zarathustra*. In R. J. Hollingdale (Trans.). London, New York: Penguin Books, 1961.

Nietzsche, F. (1886). *Beyond Good and Evil*. In R. J. Hollingdale (Trans.). London, New York: Penguin Books, 1973.

Plato. (1942). *Phaedo*. In B. Jowett (Trans.). *Five Great Dialogues* (pp. 83–153). New York: Walter J. Black, Inc.

Reiner, A. (2002). *Beyond Rhyme & Reason*. Lancaster, CA: Red Dance Floor Press.

Reiner, A. (2009). *The Quest for Conscience and the Birth of the Mind*. London: Karnac.

Rumi. (2003). *Rumi, The Book of Love*. In C. Barks (Trans.). New York: Harper.

Segal, H. (1981). Notes on symbol formation. In *The Work of Hannah Segal: A Kleinian Approach to Clinical Practice* (pp. 49–68). New York: Jason Aronson.

Chapter 7

Infant trauma in poems and clinical work

Infant Joy

"I have no name:
I am but two days old."
What shall I call thee?
"I happy am,
Joy is my name."
Sweet joy befall thee!
    (Blake, 1789, p. 36)

Infant Sorrow

My mother groand! My father wept.
Into the dangerous world I leapt:
Helpless, naked, piping loud;
like a fiend hid in a cloud.
Struggling in my father's hands,
Striving against my swaddling bands,
Bound and weary I thought best
To sulk upon my mother's breast.
                    (Blake, 1794b, p. 42)

We see here the duality of emotional experiences that abound, dualities of good and bad, of joy and sorrow, which raise the question of how these are to be resolved. Blake was particularly attuned to the emotional experiences of the child, and 100 years later, in Rilke's grand poetic opus, *Duino Elegies,* he also addressed the critical importance of childhood to one's view of life.

Don't suppose that fate's any more than childhood's density.
                                        (Rilke, 1978, p. 64)

DOI: 10.4324/9781003470953-8

It is much more typically the psychoanalyst's job to unpack that density of early emotional life. One's very fate is determined by those feelings, and by the primal, usually erroneous "conclusions" that are reached by very young children, long before they are even able to think. It may take decades to help a traumatized child or infant that is buried under his or her own misconceptions, still hidden within the psyche of the adult patient. It may take years, first to reveal that a more essential self has not yet been psychically born, and even longer for that self to feel safe enough to emerge. Having previously written about Rilke's uncanny insights into that "childhood density" in his Seventh Elegy, and that work as a whole, I will not revisit his work here (cf., Reiner, 2012). In this chapter, we will look at poems by William Blake and Giacomo Leopardi, two other poets who were extremely sensitive to the experiences of children and infants. Their perceptions, in the 18th and 19th centuries, respectively, reflect emotional aspects of primitive mental life with which psychoanalysts today are trained to work, although Blake wrote more than a century before Freud, and it was not until almost a century *after* Freud that this deeply intuitive level of infant mental experience gained acceptance in psychoanalysis. One exception to this was the work of Sándor Ferenzci, whose revolutionary insights into the emotional life of the infant in the 1920s and 1930s garnered enormous resistance from psychoanalytic colleagues, most notably from Freud, his analyst and mentor. Ferenczi was known by some as the "enfant terrible" of psychoanalysis (Fergusson & Gutiérrez-Peláez, 2022, p. 15), as not all of his sometimes wild experimental ideas bore fruit. Others of them, however, are now central tenets in contemporary psychoanalytic understanding of the effects of very early emotional trauma in the etiology of mental pathology (cf. Reiner, 2017). I will also briefly discuss in this chapter, his lesser known theory of the "astra," which touches upon the mystical perspective in Blake's and in Bion's works, and is in some ways consistent with Bion's concept of O.

Despite the different methods in the diverse disciplines of art, poetry, philosophy, science and psychoanalysis, what is similar is the state of mind necessary for the creative person to do his or her work in any of these fields. Each of them involves making contact with a version of the waking-dream state of O that Bion viewed as a prerequisite to clinical work in psychoanalysis. As we saw in Chapter 3, Rumi's (1993) description of the mystic or "man of God," as being "drunken while sober" (p. 60), is the same state of mind as Bion's "waking-dream state of O, which are both also reflected in Pessoa's (1931) "delight in losing myself…" (p. 9). All of these are also consistent with the description in the ancient Hindu text, *The Bhagavadgita* of the meditative knowledge of "A man of firm judgement," who "withdraws his senses from the sensual world" (p. 33). Like O, Bion's non-sense-based state of mind "without memory, desire, or understanding," these are all mental disciplines that facilitate contact with a transcendent sense of self.

Much of Emily Dickinson's work also reflects mystical intuitions. In one poem she describes her writing as, "Bulletins all Day From Immortality" (Dickinson, 1929, p. 401). Blake also described himself as "…under the direction of Messengers from Heaven" (Bredvold et al., 1956, p. 1051). Leopardi, considered to be one of the greatest poets and thinkers of his age, was often overwhelmed by his early feelings as his acute intuition that bravely plumbed the depths of his despair. In this regard, it is interesting to note Freud's admission that poets and writers could often naturally, and more easily than psychoanalysts, experience these emotional depths (Freud, 1960, p. 389). It speaks to the fact that their minds are open to that dream-like state that can reach this awareness through intuition, and cannot be as effectively reached through logic, often considered central to scientific endeavors. This is not meant to disparage either method, but it is a recognition of Bion's (1962) idea that it is necessary in psychoanalysis to use both means of mental functioning together, what he called "binocular vision" (p. 86). It is, in a sense the purpose of this book, to help us as analysts to find ways to maximize this awareness, to transcend one-dimensional vision and learn how to be, like Rumi's man of God, "drunken while sober."

William Blake – the challenges of a visionary

Blake was an 18th century visionary poet and illustrator whose extraordinary insights into the lives of children is evident in many of his poems, including those below from his book, *Songs of Innocence.*

Later in Blake's marriage, his wife said, "I have very little of Blake's company; he is always in Paradise" (Bredvold et al. 1956, p. 1051), and in the following quote, we can see some of the ways that Blake both suffered and enjoyed the life of a seer of visions. Earlier in his life he had attempted to live a "normal" life, and found employment as a printmaker for a more conventional poet. However, he soon felt stifled by this less imaginative work, and found it impossible to keep working that job. He revealed his real feelings in this letter to his patron for his own poetry.

> I am not ashamed, afraid, or averse to tell you what Ought to be Told: That I am under the direction of Messengers from Heaven, Daily and Nightly, but the nature of such things is not, as some suppose, without trouble or care. Temptations are on the right hand and left; behind, the sea of time and space roars and follows swiftly;… But if we fear to do the dictates of our Angels, and tremble at the Tasks set before us, if we refuse to do Spiritual Acts because of Natural Fears or Natural Desires! Who can describe the dismal torments of such a state!
>
> (Bredvold et al. 1956, p. 1051)

After this, Blake returned to London where he lived in relative obscurity, for he valued the wealth in his brain over the riches of fame. From an early age he saw visions, and while he was considered odd, even a madman by some, he was highly respected for his creativity. His reference here to "angels" may or may not be religious per se but seem to be what other artists in his and other times would also call the Muse, unmanifest entities that facilitate access to a mental state that is open to the messages from Heaven, like Dickinson's "Bulletins From Immortality," and Bion's O. We see something of this distinction in these two short poems from *Songs of Innocence.*

The Little Boy Lost

Father! Father! Where are you going?
O do not walk so fast.
Speak, father, speak to your little boy,
Or else I shall be lost."
The night was dark, no father was there;
The child was wet with dew;
The mire was deep, and the child did weep,
And away the vapour flew.
                        (Blake, 1789, p. 49)

The Little Boy Found

The little boy lost in the lonely fen,
Led by the wand'ring light,
Began to cry; but God, ever nigh,
Appear'd like his father, in white.
He kissed the child, and by the hand led,
And to his mother brought,
Who in sorrow pale, thro' the lonely dale,
Her little boy weeping sought.
                        (Blake, 1789, p. 50)

Is this lost, vaporous little boy in the first poem, found by God in the second poem? Blake's spiritual mysticism seems to have been a source of relief from the deep suffering he sees in children, or in his own child self, and perhaps the pain suffered in the care of a flawed or absent earthly father was felt to be redeemed by a heavenly father. From this perspective Blake's God may seem to be like the idealized father of Freud's definition of God, but we also know that while Blake was influenced by the Bible, he had no real use for organized religion. It is possible then that for him, "God" represented the more transcendent god that Symington (1994) called the "true god," an internal product of "mature religion," as opposed to Symington's notion of "the false god" of "primitive religion." The latter sees God as an omnipotent, external force (p. 119), which fits into Freud's idea of God as the idealized father and religion as an infantile neurosis. However, Symington's distinction reflects what Bion and Eckhart described as the "Godhead," a mature or secular religion concerned with developing one's own sense of godhood. Like the Gnostic view, it reflects a personal experience of divine knowledge that must be learned and developed by each person, as distinct from the traditionl belief, or primitive religious notion, of an external, anthropomorphic God. Blake early on already had his own conduit to transcendent visions, so it again seems likely that his description of the lost boy in the second poem, "led by the wand'ring light," is of someone already on his own quest for divine knowledge. For our purposes, it is a way of understanding the differentiation Bion made about O, distinguishing it from traditional religion.

Ferenczi as pioneer infant emotional life

Sándor Ferenczi's profound insights into infantile mental life, as early as the 1900s and into the 1930s, were based on his own troubled childhood with a depressed and neglectful mother. His ideas allowed for a deeper understanding of previously uncharted territory, which were at times disturbing to Freud, his analyst and mentor. Although greatly admired by Freud, who earlier on saw Ferenczi as his potential psychoanalytic heir, Freud's inability to understand or support his controversial insights into infantile mental life eventually destroyed their relationship. He viewed them as part of Ferenzci's own regressive states of mind, and while this was probably true to some extent, it was also true that Ferenczi's (1932) ideas were innovative, and may have stimulated Freud's fear of these unfamiliar primitive feelings.

Some of Ferenczi's views of early infancy, like his perspective on what he called "the exorbitant importance of the mother," greatly influenced the work of Melanie Klein, who was Ferenczi's analysand (Fortune, 2002, p. 49). What now seems so obvious to us today, was revolutionary then, and at odds with Freud's ideas about the primary influence of the father. Despite Freud's limitations in understanding more primitive mental states, it was Freud's analytic technique that provided Ferenzci a path into studying these early mental states in his patients and himself. Another of his important, but little studied ideas of earliest infantile life, is what he called "the astra."

Ferenczi and the occult

Ferenczi described early emotional traumas of infants whose mothers, like his own, were ill, depressed, absent or neglectful. He postulated that serious emotional trauma in infancy led the child to seek solace elsewhere, in what was essentially an emotional flight to what he called the "astra," meaning the stars, where the bereft infant sought an intuitive, heavenly connection to compensate for the lack of connection to the mother. One of the things Ferenczi noticed in patients such as these, was the presence of hyper-intuitive, even mystical, paranormal and clairvoyant capacities, and he hypothesized that the etiology of these psychic "gifts" developed in response to these problematic relationships to emotionally absent mothers. He described these infants as "wise babies," for they exhibited such highly intuitive states, and he himself was surely one of those wise babies (Ferenczi, 1932, p. 81).

This is reflected in the intuitive waking-dream state of Bion's O, for according to Ferenczi (1932), the fetus or neonate exists in a "still half-dissolved state, with an imaginative mind in 'much closer contact with the universe'" (p. 81). However, the infant's half-asleep, unconscious state *differs essentially from Bion's idea of O as the necessary psychoanalytic vertex* (Bion, 1970). I have written about this in more detail elsewhere, and essentially found that the psychic gifts of these "wise babies" who possess uncanny knowledge, were also accompanied by states of detachment and fragmentation (Reiner, 2017). In similar cases with my own patients, I saw that as adults they lacked the foundation of a self or a mind, for having so early mentally fled from the mother, and from their own feelings of pain, love, hate and confusion, they did not have the opportunity for a self to develop. Whatever they gleaned intuitively could not, therefore, really be known, for there was no mind or self to know it, and so it cannot be used in mental development.

As briefly mentioned in Chapter 6, despite Freud's own keen interest in matters of the occult, he advised Ferenczi not to publish his ideas on the subject, for he feared that it would tarnish the scientific reputation of psychoanalysis. Ferenczi did, however, present his paper, "Confusion of tongues between adults and the child" at the XIIth Congress of Psychoanalysis in 1932, and while Freud was ill and did not attend, he had a negative reaction to the paper, and to its being presented (Fergusson & Gutiérrez-Peláez, 2022, p. 76). Ferenczi, and his work, were in a way ostracized, and Ernest Jones withheld its publication, despite his earlier promise that it would be published in the next *International Journal of Psycho-analysis* (Fergusson & Gutiérrez-Peláez, 2022, p. 5). In fact, the paper would not be published for another sixteen years. Aside from Jung, Ferenczi was one of the few, before Bion, to address any of these mystical states in psychoanalysis.

The negative reactions to Bion's (1965) introduction of the mystical O into psychoanalysis makes Freud's earlier hesitation about introducing such topics seem warranted. But there are distinctions, as suggested above, between Ferenczi's "astra" and Bion's O. To further clarify the differences, Ferenczi's "wise babies" were motivated by a mental escape from the pain of their problematic connections to an ill or neglectful mother, and through their own emotional detachments, they went seeking for what became an intuitive attachment to an idealized, universal "mother." This flight from the mother was also a flight from the infant's own mind, which is essentially opposite to the use Bion suggests for these deeper intuitive states in psychoanalysis. The analyst's attempt to contact that transcendent experience can only be achieved if there is a foundation for the personality, a sense of self, for it is difficult, or rather impossible, to transcend a self if there is no self. This is both the danger faced by those "wise babies," whose flights from emotional life are essentially dissociative states, and the reason Bion (1970) warned analysts of the risk of ego regression if one attempts contact with that non-sense-based creative and intuitive mind before having had one's primitive anxieties analyzed.

Leopardi and the infant mind

Giacomo Leopardi is an early 19th century Italian poet whose haunting, and often haunted poems, reveal the painful feelings of this highly sensitive but sickly child. He lived a life of unrequited love, most likely starting with his relationship to an austere and unemotional mother (Barnes, 1997, p. xi). He is a very different kind of poet from Blake, perhaps in part because Blake's mystical beliefs gave him solace for whatever emotional pain he too must have endured as a child. I don't think Leopardi ever found such solace, except perhaps in his ability to express all of this in his poems. In the classical restraint and intensity of his work, Leopardi was a Romantic poet, and yet he was decidedly post-Romantic in his characteristic of pessimism and existential pain.

This first excerpt from Leopardi's poem, "Memories," speaks of an almost eerie mixture of dread and nostalgia generated by memories of his childhood home.

Memories

I was doomed to waste my life in this
Barbarous placed where I was born,
Surrounded by a crowd of crude know-nothings...
I spend years—loveless, alone, buried alive...
And lacking all joy, it's youth I lose,
The one and only flower that blooms
In this desert we call life.

(Leopardi, 1997, p. 41)

The last three lines reveal the poet's belief that the inherent joy of youth, the one thing of value in life, is now overlaid with despair. However, the idea of a "price-less youth" that has taken flight, may be more like nostalgia for a youth he idealized but never actually had, a yearning for a wish or a dream that for him was never real. Perhaps it also reflects the inherent knowledge of what one needs, a proto-mental knowledge of the infant, similar to what Bion (1963) described as a "pre-conception" (p. 23). He describes it as the inherent expectation of a loving, giving mother, a proto-mental dream that must meet with the real experience of such a mother, in order to bring about a mental conception. He described it in part-object terms as a kind of instinctual, precognition of a nipple that could fill the emptiness of the infant's hungry mouth, which then becomes a concept when this connection is actually realized in the relationship with the mother.

For Leopardi, and sadly many others, it is not only youth that is lost, but the opportunity to experience one's *life* at all. As Bion's theories of thinking tell us, without a mother receptive to one's infant feelings, no self or mind can develop that can experience the feelings, and think them. What is really lost then is a life that can never begin, the spectral loss of which lives like a shadow within. To use Winnicott's (1960) term, a "False Self" takes over, so "the infant lives, but lives falsely" (p. 146). According to Winnicott, the main function of this False self, "is to hide the True Self" (Winnicott, 1960, pp. 146–147). Of course, that true self is hidden from the child as well who has no access to his or her real life, self or mind.

I have written quite a bit about this kind of mental "death" that occurs in the infant whose feelings and essential spirit are not received or known by the object (Reiner, 2009). What is lost then, as Leopardi experienced, is one's sense of humanness, life without purpose or joy. The nothingness of that deadened self is replaced by a proto-memory of what is instinctively expected, or a phantasy, an imagined memory of a time of meaning now lost. Again, for such a child, losing one's youth is not just the actual loss of the actual years of one's childhood, but the loss of one's *potential* to have had a childhood, or to have an adulthood, because of the essential loss of the potential for a mind or self that imbues one's life with meaning. If, as Bion says, we have an instinctual drive toward truth, it means we are driven to develop that mind or self that is capable of accommodating truth and reality, which first and foremost includes the truth of one's own existence. Just as animals, including humans, are driven to be fed, and programmed to follow the other instinctual life forces of each species, this inherent human need for truth is nonnegotiable. This enormous promise of the human mind to work toward transcendent truth is a fundamental part of what provides the joy and hope associated with that first blush of life. This untarnished hope of having a self that can connect with another self in the service of mental development, the need to be seen and known so that one can see and know one's self, is synonymous with being seen, known and loved, a prerequisite to being able to love.

I think it is that hope of connection that Leopardi calls the "one and only flower that blooms in this desert we call life," but for one whose first "love" was unrequited, he seemed to have learned very early on that this potential for a self was lost to him. We see this in another poem in which Leopardi wonders whether he would be happier if he could fly over clouds, presumably soar like a bird above his troubles. But he then adds that whatever one's circumstances, perhaps it is impossible to escape.

[Whether]Lair of beast or baby's cradle—
To that creature being born
Its birth day is a day to mourn.
                        (Leopardi, 1997, p. 63)

Leopardi's despair is echoed in the dire message expressed over a century later by Samuel Beckett, another unflinching existential writer, in this line from *Waiting For Godot*,

They give birth astride of a grave, the light gleams for an instant, then it's night once more."

                        (Beckett, 1952, p. 470)

For Beckett, this also reflected the loss of his youth, and perhaps the nostalgia for what never existed or, as he said, existed for just one hopeful instant in the inherent joy of an infant who arrives ready to be received. Like Leopardi, Beckett also found himself with a depressed and emotionally unreceptive mother, unable to provide the love that her extraordinarily sensitive child needed (Bair, 1978). In that failure to be received, the joy of hope is extinguished, as the False Self begins its masquerade of a True Self that can never fully be born. The joy that exists from the beginning of life is founded in the inherent expectation that one will be received, emotionally held, like the proto-mental knowledge that Bion sees as existing in us before we are born. The infant's inherent preconception of a nipple that will meet the needs of the baby's hungry mouth is part of our evolutionary birthright, an *a priori* desire and an expectation that cannot be thought but whose failure nonetheless results in a dying of the soul, unconsciously suffered throughout one's life.

Clinical example of primitive mental states

This clinical example of a recent session with "Beth," reveals just how real, and enduring, the consequences of these early failures are. Beth is an extremely sensitive person, whose mother was a well-intentioned and loving person, but was also emotionally detached. Her own mother had grown up in foster care and so she too was unable to develop her own emotional life, or be present emotionally for Beth, who had been anxious her whole life. At three months, her mother's milk was insufficient and when she developed an abscess on her nipple, her mother weaned her. Beth had already been underfed, and probably working very hard to get what she needed from the breast. Growing up, she felt everything intensely, but had no way to know what she was feeling. This session was eight years into her analysis, and she had recently become involved with "Bill," a man she very much liked but who had recently become abruptly unavailable. Last session Beth was having trouble concentrating on work, which was unusual for her, and I had interpreted that she seemed not to be aware of how sad she felt about Bill's absence. In today's session she was more engaged, and said, "I can't believe how much grief I have… I guess you were right, I wasn't feeling it." She also reported having gotten inspired to work, and had done some creative writing. She told me her dream from last night.

> I was on a sled in the snow with someone, I don't know who it was. I saw a family that looked like Eskimos, and I saw a little girl running away from them. There were dogs there I think… maybe to drive the sled… Then in another part of the dream Bill was there, and we both agreed that we need to rewrite… or revise… the story of our relationship.

Beth described the sled as "a sleigh like the one Santa Claus had," and she had thoughts of Christmas as a joyful time in her family. She then said, "I thought in the dream, 'Dr. Reiner is going to say that the little girl is me, who is running away from my mother.'" I was surprised by this, for although I had interpreted on several occasions that she seemed to have run away from home emotionally, and had then lived a life of exile in an attempt to avoid these feelings of abandonment, this had remained largely unconscious. However, she had never inserted an interpretation from me into her dream, and it amused her. She then mentioned that she was reading a novel about people in Lappland, where there was lots of snow. The father of a little girl in the book had suffered a serious illness, which she put together with the fact that Bill had also recently suffered a similar illness. While he was okay, just as their relationship was starting, it seemed to have ended.

I interpreted that her grief about Bill's disappearance was another version of her feelings about "losing" her mother in infancy, for despite her on-going presence in Beth's life, her mother had similarly "disappeared" emotionally, leaving Beth alone, grieving and cold, as she was now. I said, "Because there was no way for you to know what your grief was about as a baby, you kept running away from the grief, and it seems that even your mother didn't know that something was seriously bothering you."

In trying not to feel her grief about Bill, Beth had again detached from herself and her feelings but this cold, snowy environment in her dream reflected the coldness she had always felt inside, despite her loving home, and joyful family Christmases. I thought that the unknown girl with her in the sleigh also reflected her interpretation that she attributed to me in the dream, that she was the little girl in the dream who had run away. And so this little girl sitting next to her was also her child self that, as she said, she didn't know. There was a joyful, lively Beth, but this other aspect of her that was a sad, cold little girl, was unknown to her, who did not know what was wrong.

Like Leopardi, Beth had spent her childhood, "loveless, alone, buried alive," but her connection to me in her dream indicated that she now trusts that I know about this cold little girl, and so she can know something about her too, and is no longer quite so lost.

Beth's next association seemed to confirm this, for she told me that a good friend had come to visit her yesterday, and she had shared with him that she was feeling sad. This was uncharacteristic of her, and he replied, "Sounds like you need a hug," to which she replied, "Now you're going to make me cry." He did give her a hug, and she did cry, which was different from that little girl self in cold exile, for her openness here was rewarded by his warmth. I said that as a child she had probably gotten lots of hugs from her mother, but because she had already "run away" emotionally, she was not really there to receive them, and so she continued to feel unloved. This resonated with her deeply, and we could both feel that something was different. It had taken years. Although Beth's dreams had sometimes been fragmented and hard for me to read, especially when she was detached from her feelings, this one seemed unusually clear. I felt that she was not only present for her friend's hug, but also was unusually present in the session with me. In addition, she had never before dreamt of me directly in her dreams, but she seemed to have felt my presence with her in her dream. Her early, and completely unconscious fear of closeness and love, had led to a lifetime of repetitions of that early abandonment, which she may have felt, but knew nothing about.

Proto-mental knowledge

Beth's experience reflects Bion's idea of proto-mental knowledge, a kind of *a priori* knowledge of something present in the mind which cannot be known as there was no mind yet to think it. It is related to Jung's idea of universal archetypes, and the collective unconscious, which was felt by Jung to be "everything that precedes the personal history of the human being" (Jung, 1977, p. 231). When asked about Jung's archetypes, Bion replied:

> I think he was probably talking about the same thing. There exists some fundamental mind…that seems to remain unaltered in us all.
>
> (Bion, 1978, p. 4)

It reflects an inherent evolutionary promise about what it means to be human, and as we saw in the example of Beth, the infant seems to have a clear, although unconscious, sense of how things should be, and a concurrent sense, also unconscious, that if things are *not* as they should be, that something is terribly wrong. Most infants "know" what they need, and they need to have it, or there will most likely be serious, if hidden developmental consequences, in the child's mental life.

Both Beckett's and Leopardi's stern, emotionally detached mothers were unable to hold the spirits or emotional selves of their unusually sensitive children. None of this is meant to blame mothers who cannot fulfill this emotional task, for it reflects a general lack of knowledge about the breadth and depth of the emotional life of the infant, whose extreme vulnerability often translates into uncompromising emotional needs. These are often unintentional traumas, which nonetheless can leave these infants bereft of the main thing of value in life. The human mind is inherently moral and "scientific," always looking for ways to understand what is not understood, and the infant mind is no exception. Fairbairn's (1943) moral defense predicts that they will be looking for someone to blame, and will take turns blaming their mothers, and themselves. This can lead to a lifetime of confusion between who and what are good or bad. The problem is not finding who is blameworthy, but rather how to find a way out of that primitive split between good and bad. Religion may blame Satan and seek salvation in God, but this does not help any more than finding one's mother or oneself to be Satan incarnate, or the second coming of Christ. Neither is true or useful, for an identification with God divests one of the possibility of developing one's own integrated mind.

Later in Leopardi's poem, "Memories," he writes of his great hopes and the "childish enchantments" to which he continuously returns. He implies that these are memories but which, as discussed. are probably already rewritten "memories" designed to uplift and enchant his spirit to render the intolerable tolerable. This essentially universal defense relies on the infant's imagination to recreate reality. Leopardi called them, "changes of heart," for it does indeed alter the bleak emotional landscape, but it is these distortions of reality to which he returns, and it is these re-created "memories" that never happened, that he cannot forget. He writes:

My life is wretched, my days and nights
Nothing but a blank... But
Whenever I think of you, old hopes and
golden dreams of youth...
Not one of these high hopes left but death—
I feel my heart slam shut...
                              (Leopardi, 1997, p. 43)

These distortions of reality only serve to repeat the disappointment in finding that his beautiful lie is not real. His wretched existential sadness, replaced by these "memories" that are not memories, are created to comfort him, but as we see it does not work. While those lovely memories of youth are fiction, they are created of an archetypal hope, unremembered but never abandoned, of what life should have been.

In excerpts from this one last poem by Leopardi, he writes that a man comes into the world filled with pain and suffering, but the message of the poem is something of an anomaly for Leopardi, in that the parents are depicted as doing all they can to console their suffering child, offering support, kindness and consolation for the inevitable pain of existence. The poet then asks:

But why bring into the light of day,
Why protect the life of a creature
Who needs to be consoled for life?
If life is nothing but misfortune,
What's the point of bearing it at all?
                    (Leopardi, 1997, p. 59)

Why be born at all, he seems to ask, why bring a child into this world? Leopardi's pessimistic view of the human condition is an unflinching look at existential despair, and yet in this poem he seems to be "flinching," for he views these parents as helpful and consoling when in fact he felt so neglected and invisible in his home. We can only conjecture about these emotional dynamics since I don't know the specific circumstances to which he alludes, but as inevitable as human suffering is, it seems equally inevitable for the child to want to recreate the image of the parents, in much the way that Fairbairn described. Ferenczi (1932) first described these dynamics for infants neglected by their mothers, but Fairbairn's (1943) theory of the infant's "moral defense," alluded to above, describes in detail how the child of a sick or neglectful mother alters the reality to make it more tolerable. The infant attempts to protect his love for a "bad" mother by making her "good," but unfortunately this is done by making himself bad (pp. 65–67). Most parents, however, like those in Leopardi's poem above, hopefully do strive to alleviate their infants' pain, but in many cases, even parents who do their best to attend to their infants' needs, may not know about, or know how to deal with the emotional or existential pain that even the child knows nothing about consciously. Without an awareness of the child's internal experience, even the most well-intentioned consolations cannot console the child.

Maybe it's the idea that parents so often "do their best" to console their children, but if, as with Beth, and so many patients, the parents are not emotionally equipped to connect emotionally with the child, or with their own child feelings, their best intentions will not be enough to stave off the despair of that lost potential for connection and love that each of us is instinctually programmed to expect. Perhaps because this is unconscious, Leopardi seems to feel that life is inherently disappointing, not knowing that he has lost access to the only thing that can help him to develop his mind – Truth.

Without access to the truth of one's self, through the emotional mirror of the mother's mind, all experiences – whether painful or joyous – become cauterized, sealed off and unable to be felt. This next clinical example gives another perspective on these issues.

Clinical example – "Daniel"

"Daniel" was also abruptly weaned at four months when his parents went on vacation and left him for a month in the care of a nanny. He excelled in school, had lots of friends and went on to have a satisfying career. By all accounts, Daniel was attached to his family, but his parents divorced when he was eight years old. His mother was depressed and infantile, and both parents were emotionally detached. After a few years of analysis we saw that he had unconsciously been plagued by anxiety and confusion that were masked by certain obsessional defenses.

Upon beginning treatment, he remembered very few dreams, but on the rare occasions when he did, they seemed amorphous, with random images that seemed unrelated, and few if any associations, all of which made it difficult to find meaning in them. This was unusual for me as I worked with dreams every day, with almost every patient, and while it is never easy, I would eventually be able to interpret them. But Daniel's dreams were different. Although he was intelligent, his dreams communicated someone who was lost, with no mind to contain his feelings, thoughts or dreams, and in a sense no dreamer to dream them. While Daniel seemed not really to know where he was, or who he was, he did not appear to be unemotional or disengaged, in fact he often seemed full of life, while his dreams revealed an underlying fragmentation, which was sometimes given a disturbing illusion of order through his obsessional thoughts and phantasies.

Despite the dense opacity of his dreams, I began to get little glimpses and could usually interpret a little something, one image or feeling in the dream. Apparently this was sufficient for some development to take place, and after two years he was aware enough of his feelings to feel, and to say, "I'm lost." After another year I noticed a significant change in his dreams, which had become somewhat more organized, and more emotionally evocative. He also had more associations, all of which made it possible to find more meaning in the dreams

Session #1

In this session, around the sixth year of analysis, Daniel came in looking glum. "I feel so sad," he said simply, but he did not know why.

> "I dreamt I was hiking on a mountain road with my parents and my [younger] brother. My brother dropped two water bottles which started rolling down the hill. I saw my mother lunge for them and she fell, I was terrified she would fall off the mountain, but she sort of rolled over and seemed okay."

He explained, "My brother didn't seem to want or need these bottles, which were empty, but since my mother apparently thought they were important, I tried to retrieve them." This was such a clear depiction of his early trauma, to the connection between his early weaning and these two empty "bottles," that he, rather surprisingly, said, "It seems so obvious."

The change in his pattern of dreaming was interesting to me, and seemed to represent a change in his mental life, which was now sometimes more organized, more in touch with feelings and more meaningful to him. It was certainly so in this dream, which was as clear as his early dreams were obscure. This kind of clarity in a dream seemed to indicate that once deeply unconscious states are now hovering closer to consciousness, or were almost conscious. I say "almost" because as Daniel said earlier, he felt very sad today but had no idea why, until he told me his dream about the two empty water bottles, and associated it with the weaning and loss of the breasts. While this early trauma had often played a part in his dreams, this was the first time it had seemed "obvious" to him.

Daniel remembered the painful childhood feeling of "never being able to get enough of my mother." His brother, he noted, didn't need as much from their mother. I agreed with him about the dream and said that it also showed the terrible danger he must have felt that his mother would die, or perhaps that she already *had* died, as the breasts, like the bottles in the dream, just disappeared from him without his knowing why. Part of this fear was linked to primitive fears of having destroyed his mother, either with his anger at being deprived, or by his fear of having devoured her. The actual deprivation was felt to be controlled by his depriving himself in years of harsh dieting, but this self-imposed deprivation keeps him attached to the depriving mother, where deprivation itself is idealized.

Daniel's feeling that he "couldn't get enough" of his mother, was an unconscious memory of that absent breast, a desperate feeling of need which made him feel like what Blake called a "fiend." Having more time with his mother, however, could never satisfy the constant unconscious yearning he didn't even know he had, and so he was not just a ravenous fiend, but "a fiend in a cloud," a hungry infant haunted by unknowable pain. In this particular dream, I thought that Daniel's brother who didn't care about the bottles, may also represent the baby Daniel, who told himself he didn't need food, or his mother, rejecting his mother, for he had no other way to process the loss. At least here, both the hungry *and* the self-depriving baby were being represented, along with the two aspects of the mother, and of me in the transference. This session oscillates between feeling the truth and denying it, for if I am his mother in the dream, I am the empty breasts, but like his mother in the dream who lunges for the bottles to keep them from rolling away, I am also a mother who knows how deprived and anxious Daniel is, and who knows that he wants and needs to eat. At the very least, it is a slightly different view of the breasts/mother who simply disappeared, as if falling off the mountain and dying in Daniel's mind.

Five months later

Daniel's tendencies to limit his eating severely are still present at times, when he tries to do away with dangerous feelings of a need he fears will not be met. Daniel recently met "Emily," a woman he likes a lot, and this relationship has aroused more vulnerable feelings of need and desire. After a particularly hurtful interaction between them in which Daniel felt abandoned, he then essentially projected those feelings onto Emily by accusing her of not being able to be vulnerable to *her* feelings. He was later tortured by guilt, and fear that he had ruined the relationship and would, once again, be abandoned. As he talked about it, however, he again became angry with Emily for having disappeared, exclaiming angrily, "She can't deal with feelings!" I pointed out that he too sometimes finds it too painful to have those old feelings of need, and I thought his confusion about this had given Emily mixed messages of wanting to be with her, then pushing her away, as he had done with his mother. He calmed down for the moment, but this kept happening throughout the session, as the ambivalent feelings now began to be played out with me in the transference. As vulnerability became intolerable, he slid into that old deprived baby state, and wanted nothing from Emily, or from me. Whatever I offered was at first wanted, but then he would again become irritated with me as that untrustworthy mother. By the end of the session I was concerned about his state of mind.

Session #2: The next day

The next day, Daniel was clearly feeling good, and reported that the pain of his guilt and loss was so unbearable that he had eventually called Emily to say how sorry he was for what he said, and for hurting her. He felt immediately better after taking responsibility for his behavior, and for having told her, and himself, the truth. He felt energized, and amazed at the power of truth to relieve his pain. Despite having thrown up roadblocks with me throughout the last session, he had apparently heard, tolerated and digested the pain of what I'd said. He had embraced what was essentially the depressive position, and discovered the value of truth, accountability and conscience. Despite his efforts to obscure the truth, he had heard it.

> I dreamt I was meeting someone in a sort of creative space… like an office space, but kind of industrial looking, concrete floors, modern architecture. Lots of people were there working on computers and things. I saw my old boss there, a nice woman, friendly, who really valued my work. But as we were talking I could also see the person I was there to meet, standing and watching us talk.

This dream seemed very opaque to me. Daniel had some associations to his old job, and former boss, of whom he was very fond. He did not know whom he was meeting there but thought it was a woman. "It wasn't Emily," he said, then added, "I woke up thinking about Emily, but I had an uncomfortable feeling… I don't know how to describe it… sad, but kind of weird, like something dark or obscure."

I still had no idea what the dream meant, but I commented that at this point his relationship with Emily was in fact obscure, since they barely know each other yet. He said, "I don't even really know how available she is." While he meant, in part, that he didn't know if she was involved with someone else, I thought that clearly the same goes for him, he doesn't really know yet just how available he is for a relationship, as caring about someone activates such an old and unmanageable fear of abandonment.

At that point it seemed to me that much of what he said about the dream had to do with this "industrial space," a "work space." It then struck me that what he is talking about here is finally getting a sense of a space where work can take place. This is in part our work space, his ability to work with me, to hear me, which is only possible because he now also has a new "work space" in his own mind, a "work space" that is the beginning of his own mind or self. Into this space, also come feelings and thoughts that are ungrounded, that keep jettisoning him back to the past, like his experience of the last session, in which he kept trying to escape our "work space." While he resisted my continued efforts to get him back, he was eventually able to hear the painful things I said to him last session. His subsequent apology to Emily was evidence of this, as was his ability to engage in actual thinking again. This differs from the activity of running aimlessly through old feelings *as if* he were thinking, but with no real mental space in which to work.

This dream helped to crystallize my experience with Daniel. Prior to this, and despite Daniel's desire to work in analysis, he did not yet really know how to work. There was sometimes an underlying feeling of obstruction, of not quite being able to get him into the room, but this dream was unconscious acknowledgment of a new, industrial and industrious, possibility in our relationship. About the unknown woman he was there to meet, I said, "Maybe that is me, but I think maybe it is us, that a part of you can now stand by and watch us work together." I said that I thought he had just gotten the idea that he needs this work space in his mind if we are going to sort out the confusion of the past, to which he keeps running for answers out of fear, and habit. In fact, there are no answers there, just the sadness and disappointment of his undigested loss, and his anxiety that it is about to happen all over again.

Summary and conclusions

Nostalgia for the past can be a form of depression, looking back to what seemed like a better time, perhaps because one has already survived it. However, as we see with Beth, Daniel and with Leopardi, nostalgia can be a habitual retreat to the apparent safety of a past one thought one had successfully transformed into a more pleasing "memory." Daniel's last session reveals how difficult it is to replace that tendency to recreate one's past through imagination, which instead creates a past that can never really change. The lovely distortions of truth are amorphous phantasies that cannot be thought about if there is still no mind, no "work space" in which to think them.

Those like Leopardi, and these patients, have lost everything, exiled from their own incipient minds. What seems like nostalgia for the past may not only be nostalgia for the lost years of an actual childhood, but the much greater loss of an archetypal promise of what it means to be human – to have a real self or mind – without which one cannot really have one's life. Psychoanalysis can be painstaking and slow, but in Daniel's case, we can see that what is required is the creation of a mental space which can accommodate Truth, that facilitates the work of thinking.

References

Bair, D. (1978). *Samuel Beckett: A Biography*. New York: Harcourt, Brace, Jovanovich.

Barnes, J.C. (1997). Introduction to *Leopardi: Selected Poems* (pp. xi-xv), Princeton, New Jersey: Princeton University Press.

Beckett, S. (1952). Waiting for Godot. In R. W. Seaver (Ed.), *I Can't Go On, I'll Go On* (pp. 367–476). New York: Grove Press, 1986.

Bion, W. R. (1962). A theory of thinking. In *Second Thoughts* (pp. 110–119). New York: Jason Aronson, 1967.

Bion, W. R. (1963). *Elements of Psychoanalysis*. New York: Basic Books.

Bion, W. R. (1965). Transformations. In *Seven Servants* (pp. 1–183). New York: Jason Aronson, 1977.

Bion, W. R. (1970). *Attention and Interpretation*. London: Karnac.

Bion, W. R. (1978). *Four Discussions with W.R. Bion*. Perthshire: Clunie Press.

Blake, W. (1794a). *The Norton Anthology of English Literature, Fourth Edition,* Volume 2. New York, London: W.W. Norton & Company, 1962.

Blake, W. (1794b). Infant Sorrow. In M. H. Abrams (Ed.). *The Norton Anthology of English Literature*, Fourth Edition, Volume 2 (p. 42). New York, London: W. W. Norton & Company, 1979.

Blake, W. (1789). Infant Joy. In M. H. Abrams (Ed.). *The Norton Anthology of English Literature*, Fourth Edition, Volume 2 (p. 36). New York, London: W. W. Norton & Company, 1979.

Bredvold, A.; McKillop, A.; Whitney, L. (Eds.) (1956). *Eighteenth Century Poetry and Prose,* Second Edition. New York: The Ronald Press Company.

Dickinson, E. (1929). In T. H. Johnson (Ed.). *The Complete Poems of Emily Dickinson*. New York, Boston, London: Back Bay Books/Little Brown and Company, 2022.

Fairbairn, W. R. D. (1943). The repression and the return of bad objects (with special reference to the 'War Neuroses'. In *Psychoanalytic Studies of the Personality* (pp. 59–81). Hove and New York: Brunner-Routledge, 1952.

Ferenczi, S. (1932). In J. Dupont (Ed.), M. Balint; N. Z. Jackson (Trans.). *The Clinical Diary of Sándor Ferenczi*. Cambridge, MA: Harvard University Press, 1985.

Fergusson, A., & Gutiérrez-Peláez, M. (2022). *Sándor Ferenczi: A Contemporary Introduction*. Abingdon, Oxon: Routledge.

Fortune, C. (Ed.) (2002). *Sándor Ferenczi, Georg Groddeck Correspondence: 1921–1933*. London: Open Gate Press.

Freud, E. (Ed.) (1960). *Letters of Sigmund Freud, 1873–1939*. In T. Stern; J. Stern (Trans.). New York: Basic Books.

Jung, C. G. (1977). *C.G. Jung Speaking: Interviews and Encounters*. In W. McGuire; W. F. C. Hull (Eds.). Princeton, NJ: Princeton University Press, Bollingen Series XCVII.

Leopardi, G. (1997). Memory. In E. Grennan (Trans.). *Leopardi: Selected Poems*. Princeton, NJ: Princeton University Press.

Pessoa, F. (1931). In A. Mac Adam (Trans.) *The Book of Disquiet*. Boston, Massachusetts: Exact Change, Pantheon Books, a division of Random House, Inc.., 1998.

Reiner, A. (2009). *The Quest for Conscience and The Birth of the Mind*. London: Karnac.

Reiner, A. (2012). *Bion and Being: Passion and the Creative Mind*. London: Karnac.

Reiner, A. (2017). Ferenczi's 'Astra' and Bion's 'O': A Clinical Perspective. In A. Reiner (Ed.). *Of Things Invisible to Mortal Sight: Celebrating the Work of James S. Grotstein* (pp. 131–148). London: Karnac.

Rilke, R. M. (1978). In D. Young (Trans.) *Duino Elegies,* Seventh Elegy (pp. 61–69). New York: W. W. Norton & Company.

Rumi (1993). *Love Is A Stranger*. In K. Helminski (Trans.). Putney, VT: Threshold Books.

Symington, N. (1994). *Emotion and Spirit: Questioning the Claims of Psychoanalysis and Religion*. London: Karnac Books.

Winnicott, D. (1960). Ego distortion in terms of true and false self. In M. Masud R. Khan (Ed.).*The Maturational Process and the Facilitating Environment* (pp. 140–152). London: Karnac, 1965.

Chapter 8

Poems of being, poems of O

Although the metaphysical world of dreams and imagination may seem insubstantial compared to the physical world of everyday life, our dreams carry the strength to fuel the best achievements of mankind. The images and events that are brought together in our dreams may seem nonsensical to our logical minds, but these idiosyncratic unions with our dreaming minds give rise to art, new ideas and scientific discoveries. While someone may be considered mad for believing in fairies, mythological and literary inventions of fairies and sprites provide ways to talk about metaphysical experiences that cannot otherwise be described in logical language. As analysts, we interpret the individual "myths" of a person's dreams, and I have seen all sorts of vaporous winds and mysterious alien beings stand for someone's spirit, or for their unthought thoughts, for our own thoughts or feelings are also insubstantial and invisible flights of fancy. In one writer's dream, a disembodied spirit symbolized a new idea that had come to him, a creative idea that suddenly had "wings," and which, when interpreted, he could then think about, and use, as his imagination was released to write a new play. Although thoughts and ideas are without substance or physical manifestation of any kind, we can then give form in a sculpture, a new thought or a brave deed, while also contributing to our own mental growth. As Shakespeare writes in *The Tempest*, we *are* our dreams.

> *Our revels now are ended. These our actors,*
> *As I foretold you, were all spirits, and*
> *Are melted into air, into thin air...*
> *Yea, all which it inherit, shall dissolve,*
> *And like this insubstantial pageant faded,*
> *Leave not a rack behind. We are such stuff*
> *As dreams are made on, and our little life*
> *Is rounded with a sleep.*
> (Shakespeare, 1623, p. 37)

If, as Bion said, dreams are part and parcel of our capacity to think about, and feel, our experiences, to digest them emotionally and render them capable of being remembered, our very beings are indeed dependent on and composed of dreams.

The rest of this chapter consists primarily of poems that I wrote, some recently and others from my earlier books of poetry. Having probably already said too much in an

DOI: 10.4324/9781003470953-9

attempt to explain things that are ultimately inexplicable, it is time to let some poems speak for themselves, so the reader has a chance to *feel* these states of mind rather than only *think* about them, to feed the dreaming part of our minds. They reflect ideas throughout this book, including, of course, the state of mind of Bion's O. Other poems are contemplations on the mental states of being and nonbeing, like the immersion in the experience of being that Pessoa described as his need to "lose himself" (above, Chapter 5), and where what seems like non-being reflects a deeper experience of being. While I have never set out to write poems about any of these subjects, apparently these things are on my mind, and emerge by silencing that ego-self and entering an ephemeral present that can be captured for a moment, before it slips away again like a dream.

In short, no one can fully understand the infinite, unconscious mind, or the poems born of that mind, whose messages are embedded in words that play with other words in ways that prosaic words of logic generally do not. Their messages, like the messages of dreams, are as ephemeral as words written in wet sand at high tide, the ocean always ready to wash them away. Keats, who died young in February of 1921, famously had the following words etched on his gravestone in Rome's Protestant Cemetery, "Here lies One Whose Name was writ in Water." (Stacey, 2016). While there is some controversy as to the intended meaning of his epitaph I think it reflects both the ephemeral nature of poetry, and of life, as well as the frustrated legacy of a writer who devoted his life to poetry but died at the age of 25, before his genius could reach the audience it deserved.

The idea of a name "writ in water," reflects that ephemeral dreaming self, the experience of O as the essence of an elusive moment of truth or reality, contact with which depends upon our ability to relinquish control.

The Poet's Job

Imagine
there is one Word
that can save the world –
find it.
         (Reiner, 1997, p. 5)

Zen

Nothing is more
Important
than this poem
and this poem
Is
no longer important.
         (Reiner, 1994, p. 9)

The next three previously unpublished, short poems are followed by some longer, and one much longer poem, most of which are from books I have written over the years. As with most poems, they mean what they say in whatever language they can say it, and like dreams, we may or may not understand their particular use of language.

A poem is the answer
to a question
no one ever asked.

When I fall asleep
I wake up in a dream.
When I wake up in the morning
I am asleep.

A poet is a playground
for Words
that are learning
how to play.
    (Reiner, 2023a, Unpublished)

The Art of Seeing

Look.
Seeing
is a mystery,
the answer to which may solve the riddle of the Sphinx.
Oh wait, that's already been solved.
Although even what we know
remains unknown
and so must be learned
all over again
every day in a different way
as each new Truth
tips the balance
and the world shifts
till once again we don't know it.
How much do we miss
if every answer is a step into a brand new abyss
of ignorance
out of which the only way out is
another mystery.
                    (Reiner, 1923b, Unpublished)

It is not yet enough to have memories. One must be able to forget them.... Not till they have turned to blood within us... nameless and no longer to be distinguished from ourselves – not till then can it happen that in a most rare hour, the first word of a verse arises in their midst and goes forth from them.
                    Rilke on "Blood-Remembering" (1975, p. 94)

Orange

Words are not words
so do not speak them.
Sleep with them, dream them,
dance them, or plant them so
beneath each step
a poem can grow.
"Orange" is a sweet word
but do not speak it.
Squeeze it,
taste its color, its juice, then chew,
but do not speak unless you digest the sweetness
and egest the rest.
Now you can say it –
"Orange" –
because now you know what it means
to be an orange
that has passed through
and is part of you.
Speak these Words born in silence
that thrive on prayer,
you will find music there,
which only there will taste like Truth –
the sweetest fruit.
                    (Reiner, 1994, p. 28; re-edited 2016)

Freud's Pillow

I started having nightmares in that inn by the sea
with its neat garden gleaming
and the white summer sky.
They say that Freud vacationed here
and that mine was his favorite suite.
I lay in his shadow,
dreamt in his bed,
and when it was time to go –
I shouldn't have done it, I guess,
but it seemed harmless –
like taking a bar of soap or a tube of shampoo,
nothing more or less;
but since I stole Freud's pillow

I haven't had a single night's rest.
                        (Reiner, 2002, p. 24)

At the sanitorium in the Wienerwald the secret of dreams was revealed to Sigmund Freud.

Shadow

I step off the curb to cross the street,
Satan takes my hand and leads me
directly into oncoming traffic.
I smile
and shepherd him safely to the other side.
I sit down at my computer to write
but my thoughts wander
as he whispers in my ear.
I ask him please to speak up
so I can ignore him
more clearly.
                        (Reiner, 2008, p. 40)

Summary and conclusions

Eliot (1919) said, "The progress of an artist is a continual self-sacrifice, a continual extinction of personality" (p. 39). This is a succinct version of the idea of O and the creative process. Throughout this book we have talked about O as a waking-dream state that facilitates contact with a sense of the infinite, and awe, but it is also a suspension of one's ordinary sense of self, like Eliot's "extinction of the personality." From everything that has been said, it seems evident that keeping an open mind is a difficult discipline, and even a potentially dangerous one, as it can challenge our ego beliefs about what we know, and don't know, and who we are. The same challenge can be said of poetry, whose language can seem more likely than prose to pose questions than to provide answers. This was certainly true about Bion himself, who explicitly expressed his belief in our need to tolerate questions, and not knowing, if we were to learn something new. This idea was also implicit in his behavior as a teacher and lecturer, for I often saw audiences in Los Angeles who were overcome by frustration and anger because Bion did not directly answer the questions posed to him. We see this in the transcripts in his many books of lectures in Rio, New York and Sao Paulo (Bion, 1974, 1975, 1980b). Many psychoanalysts were disturbed by what they felt were Bion's vague or oblique answers to their questions, answers they thought were associative and meandering, or irrelevant and unresponsive to the question. Although I myself was also often perplexed by some of what he said, I had a very different sense of it, for while I would say that his remarks were indeed associative, it was not in a way that seemed irrelevant, disordered or unresponsive. It seemed possible that some people had missed the fact that these were relevant and coherent responses to questions that the participants themselves may not have even known they had asked, pertaining to issues they may not have known they had raised. In this regard, his responses were not unlike what an analyst does, responding not only to the *content* of a patient's associations but also to the *underlying meaning*. The following words from Francesca Bion's Preface to *Bion in New York and Sao Paulo*, underlined this same idea.

[Bion's] replies—more correctly, counter-contributions—were, in spite of their apparent irrelevance, an extension of the questions.

(Bion, 1980a, Preface)

She goes on to quote Bion as saying:

I don't know the answers to these questions—I wouldn't tell you if I did. I think it is important to find out for yourselves…

I don't think that my explanation matters. What I would draw your attention to is the nature of the problem.

(Bion, 1980a, Preface)

That which was interpreted as Bion's intention to be obscure or withholding, seemed in fact to be a disciplined effort to respond to the deeper issues behind someone's desire for what may have seemed like a simple "answer." If one thing could be said about Bion, it was that he saw the human mind as complex. His intention was to encourage people to think for themselves, rather than looking to him, or other "experts," for answers. His concept of O was very much about the need for analysts to find a way to look more deeply into their own experiences and emotional awareness. Analysts often speak of arrogance, and yet confronted with someone who refused to be put in the role of the wise sage with all the answers, Bion's humility was misinterpreted as arrogance.

Criticisms about Bion being *intentionally* obscure did not take into account the fact that the subject matter we as analysts are dealing with – namely, the human mind – is inherently obscure, and ultimately unknowable. He made it perfectly, if painfully clear, that it was misleading to pretend otherwise. Given the daunting complexity and obscurity of unconscious mental life as he depicted it, Bion may have evoked a desperate need for answers in some of his audiences, who preferred the omnipotent pretense of an expert, or a God, who had all the answers. Bion clearly did not want that job, and chose instead to remind us all that since none of us were Gods, we would have to figure things out for ourselves, a difficult and humbling job at best. In our efforts to do so, we may aspire to, and even achieve moments of integration, unity, and even godliness, but only by fully appreciating our profound limitations. We might then discover a moment of clarity, and make a cogent and effective interpretation, or write a beautiful poem, or discover a truth in whatever realm we are working. Those moments of unity are based on an awareness that our moments in the sun undoubtedly result in our being plunged back into darkness, from which we might then again discover another moment of light. It is difficult work, but like the old Gershwin song said about love, "Nice work if you can get it."

The work of analysis is sometimes uplifting, sometimes heartbreaking and sometimes evolutionary, a journey between states of enlightenment and darkness, between ignorance and knowledge that fluctuate wildly within each session and throughout a long analysis, as well as throughout our lives. Bion saw it as the on-going oscillations between Ps]D, between what he characterized in clinical work as the oscillations between patience and security. This reflects the dynamic activity of the mind itself.

I will end with the following four poems that in their own ways speak to the ideas already discussed about this inner state of nonbeing, which at times turns out to be a deeper sense of being. They address the difficulties in finding ourselves in a new way, or in a new mental space, based on intuitive dream states that go beyond our ego knowledge.

Ego-Free

Now that I'm the ocean
I don't feel wet.
I'm a book
that doesn't know it's being read,
a sky in blue and blueless flight,
I am life
that does not know it's being lived,
Time
that keeps moving, unseen,
I am empty space
for music to unfold in
and children to grow
and grow old in.
I fly so high sometimes
I have just a few falling leaves
as intermittent company,
and when they drop away
abandoned by wind,
I keep flying
the silent night.
I'm a crazy singing bird
that does not know its way,
but when it's really cold,
how – I don't know –
I always end up in Capistrano.
                    (Reiner, 2002, p. 47)

Humpty Dumpty Had a Great Fall

Humpty Dumpty didn't realize
that to fall to pieces is to write a poem,
a poem whose words, like dreams,
don't know what they're saying –
they're just dancin'! –
and those who learn to dance understand them.
After the Fall, Humpty Dumpty became a great poet,
but none of the King's horses and none of the King's men
ever understood his work.
He died, a broken egg,
unappreciated in his lifetime
but later discovered in a rare and used bookstore
when his book of poems fell off the shelf
and hit me in the head.
I was concussed
and rushed to the hospital.
When I awoke the book was there,
beside my bed,
so I read it
and was so moved
I fell to pieces.

(Reiner, 2002, p. 13)

Where Are We on the Road to Salvation?

Is this the End of the Beginning
or the Beginning of the End?
Are we in the Middle?
And if so, of what?
And does it really matter?
Wherever we are, we are Here
though where that is is not exactly clear,
and wherever we go from Here
is determined by where we once Were
which will never again be Now.
Okay, but the sky is clearly Up
and the ground is clearly Down,
except beneath that ground
is a trillion light years of empty space
situated way Up Above
and Down Below
another billion trillion galaxies.

Okay, so the sky is Up and the sky is Down
in every direction Forever
Expanding Endlessly
into Places we'll never know
and can never go.
Ergo, on the road to Salvation
we are Nowhere, which is Everywhere,
and despite the nausea and dizziness
of this whole crazy business
we'd better just chill,
and maybe someday
try to read a little more physics.
                    (Reiner, 2023c, Unpublished)

The Real Me

The real me isn't really me.
The real me is a phantasy.
The real, absolutely real me is a dream
I dreamt to house my goals
and the goals of my soul
which is the real real me
that has no physical identity.
But the real me is not un-real,
it is not a false me
or a not-me
caught in a cacophony of ghostly voices
planted like an evil seed
carried on a chilly wind
because it had no choice.
No. What is real, really, has its own song
carried on warm xylophonic winds
in the percussive thunder of love
that no one can put asunder.
Your parents gave you their seeds,
they gave you their DNA
all those things they couldn't help giving you
for that was their job and they did it that fateful day,
so thank them and send them on their way.
The you they made was just a place saver
someone to be for the time being,
before being re-schooled
in the ways of an enigmatic Lord of Being
that has no actual being.

Now is the time to shine,
to be the kind of Me I never dared to dream of,
someone you might not recognize with your eyes
but you might see it like you see the sky
which looks blue
but isn't.
This sky in the science of dreams,
is a scattering of electromagnetic waves
with which we always
and unknowingly interact
in this opalescent miracle of facts.

(Reiner, 2025, Unpublished)

References

Bion, F. (Ed.) (1980a). Preface. In *Bion in New York and Sao Paulo*. Perthshire: Clunie Press.

Bion, W. R. (1980b). *Bion in New York and Sao Paulo*. In F. Bion (Ed.). Perthshire: Clunie Press.

Eliot, T. S. (1919). Tradition and the individual talent. In *Perspecta*, 1982, vol. 19, pp. 36-42.

Reiner, A. (1994). *The Naked I*. Lancaster, CA: Red Dance Floor Press.

Reiner, A. (1997). *News from the Muse*. Laguna, CA: The Inevitable Press, Laguna Poets Series #60.

Reiner, A. (2002). *Beyond Rhyme & Reason*. Lancaster, CA: Red Dance Floor Press.

Reiner, A. (2008). *Presents of Mind*. Lancaster, CA: Red Dance Floor Press.

Reiner, A,. (2023a). *Three short poems*. Unpublished.

Reine, A. (1923b). *The Art of Seeing*. Unpublished.

Reiner, A. (2023c). *Where are We on the Road to Salvation?* Unpublished

Reiner, A. (2025). *The Real Me*. Unpublished)

Rilke, R. (1975). *Rilke on Love and Other Difficulties*. In J. J. L. Mood (Trans.). New York: W.W. Norton & Co.

Shakespeare, W. (1623). *The Tempest*. In H. Staunton (Ed.). *The Complete Illustrated Shakespeare, Three Volumes in One*. Volume III (pp. 1–46). New York: Park Lane, 1979.

Stacey, M. (2016). Writ in water. In *The Paris Review*, February 23, 2016. (An on-line blog at www.the parisreview.org/blog/2016/02/23/writinwater

Index

absolute truth 1, 5, 14, 28–30, 39, 42–43, 45–46, 57–59, 63, 70, 86, 94, 96, 98–99
Abstract Expressionists 86
alpha function 39
Analysis Terminable and Interminable (Freud) 13
ancient wisdom 95–102
Arp, J. 8, 86–89
art 1, 3, 40; ancient 86; Dada 86–89; grandeur of 47; Renaissance 86; sacred 63; surrealist 29
The Art of Seeing (Reiner) 123
Ashton, D. 90
authentic experience 1
authentic person 1
awe 38–39, 42, 47, 51, 90, 94, 100, 125; and infancy 43–44; religious feeling of 21; transcendent feeling of 7

Beckett, S. 29–30, 113
The Bhagavadgita 47, 57–60, 104
binocular vision 15, 34, 37, 105
Bion, F. 1, 126
Bion, W. 3–8, 86–89, 95; authentic experience 1; "catastrophic change" 71–72; concept of O 1, 3–6, 14, 15, 18, 20, 21, 28, 34–35, 39–41, 47, 55, 58, 59, 68, 70, 86–91, 101; cosmic religious experience 44; creativity and 3–6; *The Dawn of Oblivion* 21; faith 44–46, 93; fear of, and resistance to, change 63; *A Memoir of the Future* 74; memory and desire 3; "the mystic" 40, 42–43, 45; *The Past Presented* 35; "pre-conception" 109; proto-mental mind 26, 27, 99, 112–115; psychoanalysis 35–36, 100; psychoanalyst-self 35; relationship to

poetry 1–3; resistance 28; reverie and O 22, 39, 70; "selected fact" 27, 32, 86; statement about psychoanalysis 35–36; theories of thinking 22, 109; "thoughts without a thinker" 29, 37; unconscious 79, 81; unseen in 47–50; wild thoughts 46, 60, 88
Bion and Being: Passion and the Creative Mind (Reiner) 1
Blake, W. 8, 11, 64, 104–106; *Infant Joy* 103; *Infant Sorrow* 103; *The Little Boy Found* 106; *The Little Boy Lost* 106; *Songs of Innocence* 105; visionary 11, 64, 105–106
Boddhisatva Gets the News (Reiner) 53
The Book of Questions (Neruda) 10
British Psychoanalytic Society 42
Buddhist Impermanence 71–72
Buddhists 5, 12, 71–72
Burden, C. 89–90
Byrne, D. 89

Campos, A., Pessoa poetic alter-ego 75–76
Cast All Your Votes for Dancing (Hafiz) 54
Cavanaugh, P. 14
Chapel, R. 91
childish enchantments 113
Christian Gospels 21, 40, 95
clinical example 60–61; of primitive mental states 111–112
clinical vignette 31–32, 55–56, 74–75
clinical work, and infant trauma 103–119
Cognitive Behavioral Therapists 11
consciousness 96–99
cosmic religious experience 44
counterfeit coins 54–55
creativity and Bion's 'O' 3–6, 34–35

For Product Safety Concerns and Information please contact our EU
representative GPSR@taylorandfrancis.com
Taylor & Francis Verlag GmbH, Kaufingerstraße 24, 80331 München, Germany